Kweller Prep   Digital SAT
Reading Workbook

Douglas S. Kovel, Ed.M.

ISBN: 9798393656553

Contents

Unit 1: Information and Ideas

Week 1: Central Ideas and Details

Pre-Lesson Reflection Activity

Read the paragraph below, which is adapted from "A New England Nun" by Mary E Wilkins Freeman. As you read, reflect on the following questions:

    1) *What specifically do we learn about the way Louisa prepares tea in this excerpt?*
    2) *How do Louisa's neighbors seem to regard her? How do we know this?*
    3) *How does Louisa seem to treat herself? What makes you think this?*
    4) *What are some big takeaways we have about Louisa's personality?*

Louisa tied a green apron round her waist, and got out a flat straw hat with a green ribbon. Then she went into the garden with a little blue crockery bowl, to pick some currants for her tea. After the currants were picked she sat on the back door-step and stemmed them, collecting the stems carefully in her apron, and afterwards throwing them into the hen-coop. She looked sharply at the grass beside the step to see if any bad fallen there.

Louisa was slow and still in her movements; it took her a long time to prepare her tea; but when ready it was set forth with as much grace as if she bad been a veritable guest to her own self. The little square table stood exactly in the centre of the kitchen, and was covered with a starched linen cloth whose border pattern of flowers glistened. Louisa had a damask napkin on her tea-tray, where were arranged a cut–lass tumbler full of teaspoons, a silver cream-pitcher, a china sugar-bowl, and one pink china cup and saucer. Louisa used china every day-something which none of her neighbors did. They whispered about it among themselves. Their daily tables were laid with common crockery, their sets of best china stayed in the parlor closet, and Louisa Ellis was no richer nor better bred than they. Still she would use the china.*

*china: household tableware made from china, a type of porcelain.

While the passage is relatively short, we can still glean some meaningful information about Louisa. We know that Louisa is very slow, graceful, and deliberate in her movements, which we are both told directly and shown through descriptions of the way she goes about preparing tea (for example, she slowly stems the currants). She might remind you of a person you know who is extremely thorough in tasks he or she completes. You also might have picked up on the fact that Louisa treats herself well, using fine china as if she were hosting guests for a fancy event when she is simply having dinner alone. The fact that the neighbors whisper about her tells us they think she is a bit eccentric, or weird. The last two sentences might hint at the fact that some of her neighbors find her off-putting: by noting that Louisa is no richer or "better bred" than them, the narrator hints that the neighbors believe Louisa thinks she is superior to them despite having a similar upbringing to them. The last sentence makes clear that Louisa continues to engage in a behavior (using china) that her neighbors find odd, suggesting she either does not know what they think about her or is simply unbothered.

So, why did we go through this exercise? As you will see in this lesson and future ones, reading closely is essential to success on the SAT English exam. Before committing to any answer choice, it is important to read the passage carefully (luckily they are all very short!) and think about it in your own words. Now, we will talk a little bit more specifically about **detail** and **main idea** questions, applying them to test-like questions. Then it is time to quiz yourself with a drill! The most basic questions that appear on the reading portion of the SAT English exam are central idea and detail questions.

Details

Detail questions require you to locate and correctly interpret specific pieces of information in the text. These questions can vary in wording, but they will typically include some variation of **"based on the text"** or **"according to the text."**

Below are some hypothetical examples of **detail questions** you might see.
- According to the text, which of the following is true about Samir?
- Based on the text, why did the queen react with anger to her servant's request?
- According to the text, why was the sequencing of platypus DNA significant?

What all these questions have in common is that they ask you to identify specific pieces of information in a text.

> To approach detail questions, do the following:
> 1) Read the question to determine what information it is you are looking for. This can help guide your reading.
> 2) **Read the text** for general understanding, keeping in mind the detail you are trying to find.
> 3) Look at the question again and **predict the right answer** in your own words. Go back to the text as needed to locate information that will inform your prediction.
> 4) Read the answer choices carefully and see if any match your prediction. If any do, you can be more confident that answer is correct. Use the process of elimination to get rid of choices unsupported or contradicted by the passage.

The passage below is the second portion of the excerpt from the pre-lesson activity (note that on the actual SAT, passages will be no more than 150 words).
Sample 1

The little square table stood exactly in the centre of the kitchen, and was covered with a starched linen cloth whose border pattern of flowers glistened. Louisa had a damask napkin on her tea-tray, where were arranged a cut-glass tumbler full of teaspoons, a silver cream-pitcher, a china sugar-bowl, and one pink china cup and saucer. Louisa used china every day—something which none of her neighbors did. They whispered about it among themselves. Their daily tables were laid with everyday plates, their sets of best china stayed in the parlor closet, and Louisa Ellis was no richer nor better bred than they. Still she would use the china.

According to the passage, which of the following is true about some of Louisa's neighbors?
A) They regarded Louisa as a wealthy eccentric.
B) Their efforts to convince Louisa to alter her dining habits were unsuccessful.
C) They gossiped about aspects of Louisa's behavior they found atypical.
D) They hoped Louisa would invite them to her house for tea.

This is a fairly standard detail question. To approach this, let's follow our five steps.

Step 1: Identify what the question is asking.
The question wants us to indicate what is true about some of Louisa's neighbors. When we read, we will want to pay extra attention to any references to Louisa's neighbors: their behaviors, opinions, and attributes.

Steps 2 and 3: Read the text and predict possible right answers.
The question is fairly narrow in scope—it only asks about her neighbors. We are asked to use textual evidence about the neighbors in order to identify the neighbors' opinions of Louisa. Using the textual evidence, we can make a few predictions about possible answer choices.

- Louisa's neighbors do not use fine china on a daily basis, unlike her; instead, they use more common crockery and keep their finest china in the closet.
- Louisa's neighbors talk among each other about Louisa's unusual behavior (using fancy china for everyday use).
- Louisa is no richer or better-bred than her neighbors, meaning she had a similar upbringing and is of the same social class.

Step 4: Read the choices, looking for ones that match our predictions (if possible) and eliminating ones that are problematic.

Choice A might seem correct at first glance. Louisa's neighbors would likely describe her as eccentric in part because she uses fancy china. However, the text explicitly says Louisa is NOT wealthier than her neighbors, so they would probably regard her as eccentric (odd) but not wealthy.

Choice B is partially correct, as Louisa continues to use china while her neighbors do not. However, the passage does not indicate that her neighbors actually tried to convince her of anything. Rather, we just learn they talk amongst themselves.

Choice C looks good. The neighbors did gossip about Louisa, or talk about her behind her back. They specifically gossiped about a behavior they saw as atypical (unusual): using fancy china for everyday use. The neighbors, by contrast, used more common tableware and kept their best china hidden in their closets, presumably only using them for genuinely special occasions. **Choice C is correct.**

Choice D is not supported by the passage. While it could be true, we simply do not have enough evidence to suggest the neighbors hoped she would invite them over for tea.

Sample 2

With an ecological niche that includes terrestrial and aquatic environments, amphibians play important roles in ecosystems, though they are sometimes not given as much attention as species that are critically endangered or those that are valued for game hunting. Because amphibians are sensitive to changes in environments caused by disease—their skin is especially sensitive to subtle changes in levels of pollutants like UVB—some organizations have partnered with the government to monitor amphibian populations in Yellowstone National Park. Shifts in amphibian populations can often provide early indications of more widespread ecosystem threats that need to be addressed in conservation management plans. Consequently, many ecologists have urged more thorough monitoring of amphibian populations in Yellowstone.

According to the passage, why are many ecologists concerned about monitoring amphibian populations in Yellowstone?
   A) Amphibians play the most important role in maintaining the overall health of terrestrial and aquatic ecosystems.
   B) Amphibians' unique ability to quickly absorb pollutants protects other organisms.
   C) Existing efforts to conserve the park's ecosystems have failed to take into account climatic shifts that threaten other wildlife and plant life.
   D) Knowledge gleaned from studying amphibian populations can inform more effective environmental interventions.

We learn that amphibians play an important role in ecosystems and that changes in their populations are often indications of larger system-wide problems that might require solutions through conservation management plans. The right answer will likely deal with one or more of these ideas. Let's again examine each choice systematically.

Choice A seems a bit extreme. While we are told that amphibians play an important role in ecosystems, there is no evidence that they play the MOST important role in this regard. Other organisms not mentioned might be just as, if not more, important.

Choice B is a distortion that is not supported by the passage. The passage does say that amphibians are sensitive to pollutants in the environment, but there is no indication they absorb the pollutants to protect other animals.

Choice C is not supported by the passage. There is no discussion of what current conservation efforts do wrong. Maybe they do consider climatic shifts based on evidence unrelated to amphibians.

Choice D is correct. We learn that amphibians provide "early indications of more widespread ecosystem threats that need to be addressed in conservation management plans," and this is why many ecologists urge continued study of them. This shows that knowledge gained from these studies can better inform management plans (e.g., by identifying issues so that they can be addressed).

Central Ideas

Central idea questions require you to determine the main idea or main point of a passage. More informally, what is a big takeaway the author wants you to get from the passage? When trying to determine the main idea, ask yourself the following questions:
1) What words or ideas are mentioned repeatedly?
2) What is the larger idea for which the minor details provide support?
3) What is the most important idea that the author might want the audience to learn?
4) What is the general tone of the passage? Is it positive, negative, or neutral?

To answer central idea questions:
1) Read the passage, focusing on the general message.
2) Predict in your own words what you think were some of the most important ideas from the passage.
   - For **persuasive** pieces (e.g., speeches, certain poems), reflect on what broad opinion the author is trying to sway you to believe.
   - For **informative** pieces, ask yourself what the major pieces of information the author wants you to know are (e.g., a key scientific finding in a research study).
   - For **narrative** pieces, reflect on key details about the **characters** (e.g., their personality traits, values, interrelationships) or **plot** (important events or conditions that affect the characters in some way).
3) Examine the answer choices to see if any match your prediction. Eliminate any answer choices that are contradicted or unsupported by the passage. If you are left with two or more factually accurate choices, pick the one that relates to the broader point the writer is making. Some choices might present true but more minor details that help support the broader point.

Suppose you were trying to convince your friend about the benefits of stretching after lifting weights. You might mention that stretching increases flexibility, improves circulation, reduces lactic acid buildup, boosts energy, and aids in pain prevention. All of these would be examples of supporting details in service of the broader **main idea**, which is that stretching post-workout has many benefits.

Mini Activity 1

Read the situations below, each of which contains a bulleted list of supporting details. In your own words, think of a **main idea** that all of these supporting details support.

Situation 1 (Informative)

- Detail 1: Beavers construct dams and habitats in wetlands that provide homes for numerous species, increasing biodiversity.
- Detail 2: Beaver ponds act as filters that improve water quality.
- Detail 3: Beavers minimize the damaging effects of droughts in ecosystems by aiding in water storage.
- Detail 4: Beavers minimize the damaging effects of floods in ecosystems by slowing down the flow of water.
- Main Idea:_____

Situation 2 (Narrative)

The following details describe the character of Daisy in F. Scott Fitzgerald's *The Great Gatsby*.

- Detail 1: The narrator describes Daisy's voice as being "filled with money."
- Detail 2: Daisy becomes awed and cries when she sees Gatsby's expensive shirts, as she is impressed by his wealth.
- Detail 3: Daisy is described as moving "wherever people played polo and were rich together."
- Detail 4: Daisy married Tom even though she loved Gatsby more because Tom was wealthy.
- Main Idea: _____

Situation 3 (Persuasive)

The following are details from an opinion essay by a graduate student.

- Detail 1: In small classes, coursework can better be adapted to students' needs than in large classes.
- Detail 2: Instructors of smaller classes can typically provide quicker and more thorough feedback to students than can instructors in large classes.
- Detail 3: Compared to large classes, smaller classes typically foster a stronger classroom community, which can lead to more meaningful participation.
- Detail 4: Smaller classes are typically more amenable to hands-on assignments that allow students to learn by doing.
- Main Idea:_____

The first situation describes various ways that beavers help the environment. Possible main ideas are "beavers promote healthy ecosystems" or "beavers benefit the environment."

The second situation reveals some information about a character, all of which show her concern about money and wealth. Possible main ideas are "Daisy is materialistic" or "Daisy cares a lot about money."

The third situation shows specific ways that small classes can be superior to large classes. Possible main ideas are "smaller class sizes are superior to large class sizes" or "schools should consider adopting smaller class sizes when feasible."

Let's look at two more examples of test-like central idea questions.

Sample 3

While many people strive to achieve macro, or large-scale, goals—like writing a novel or running a marathon—a failure to achieve such goals in a timely manner can be demoralizing. Some researchers have found that setting micro-goals, smaller goals that can be achieved in a short time frame, can empower people to stay motivated, have increased self-confidence, and feel productive. Researchers from *Harvard Business Review* found that making minor strides in projects measurably increased people's feelings of happiness about their work: the more productive people feel along the way, the more likely they are to be creatively productive in the long-run. Thus, while striving to achieve major goals can be daunting, breaking them up into more manageable increments can prevent people from becoming discouraged when progress towards the macro-goal is slow.

What is the main idea of the text?
  A) While people often feel a small sense of pleasure from achieving incremental progress towards a larger macro-goal, they will ultimately quit if they only keep achieving micro-goals.
  B) Although some goals that people set for themselves can be difficult to achieve, setting micro-goals can have many psychological benefits.
  C) Most people's sense of self-confidence is determined by their ability to achieve minor yet ambitious goals.
  D) Setting small achievable goals for oneself is the best strategy for achieving daily happiness and resilience.

The passage discusses how while a failure to achieve large (macro) goals can be discouraging, there are many benefits of setting small-scale micro-goals. For example, they "can empower people to stay motivated, have increased self-confidence, and feel productive." People who achieve micro-goals are also more likely to feel self-satisfied and stay creatively productive. Taken together, the big idea seems to be that micro-goals have many benefits.

Choice A is incorrect because the second part of the sentence is not supported by the passage. It is also too negative in tone. Overall, this passage celebrates the advantages of micro-goals. A minimizes their importance by focusing on something bad (a failure to achieve macro-goals).

Choice B is correct, highlighting the "psychological benefits" of setting micro-goals, which include feeling more confident and self-satisfied. This matches our prediction.

Choice C is a bit too extreme. The passage never says that most people's self-confidence is determined by their ability to achieve micro-goals. Rather, many people can see boosts in self-confidence as a result of achieving them. This choice is also too narrow in that it focuses on self-confidence, which is just one of the many benefits of setting micro-goals.

Choice D is also too extreme because of the word "best." The author never states that setting micro-goals is the ***best*** way to achieve daily happiness and resilience. Rather, it is one tool that can aid in this.

Sample 4

The excerpt below is adapted from "Impressions of an Indian Childhood" by Zitkala-Sa.

Close beside my mother I sat on a rug, with a scrap of buckskin in one hand and an awl in the other. This was the beginning of my practical observation lessons in the art of beadwork. From a skein of finely twisted threads of silvery sinews my mother pulled out a single one. With an awl she pierced the buckskin, and skillfully threaded it with the white sinew. Picking up the tiny beads one by one, she strung them with the point of her thread, always twisting it carefully after every stitch. It took many trials before I learned how to knot my sinew thread on the point of my finger, as I saw her do. Then the next difficulty was in keeping my thread stiffly twisted, so that I could easily string my beads upon it. My mother required of me original designs for my lessons in beading. At first I frequently ensnared many a sunny hour into working a long design. Soon I learned from self-inflicted punishment to refrain from drawing complex patterns, for I had to finish whatever I began.

What is the main idea of the text?
  A) The process of beadwork that the narrator learned required discipline and meticulousness.
  B) The narrator enjoyed her beadwork lessons because they gave her an excuse to bond with her mother.
  C) The narrator's mom had modest expectations for her daughter's progress in the art of beadwork.
  D) The beadwork that the narrator and her mother engaged in integrated objects from the natural environment and specialized tools.

We learn that the narrator is taking beading lessons from her mother, who is very skilled at her craft. We learn that her mother works slowly and deliberately and has high expectations for the narrator. It takes the narrator a lot of practice to get proficient at her work. The main idea likely has something to do with the challenging nature of beadwork or the hard work the narrator puts in.

Choice A is correct. We do see that the narrator had to be very disciplined (she practiced often) and meticulous (thorough or detailed) in her beadwork.

Choice B is not supported by the passage. While the narrator admires her mother's work, there is no indication she is looking for an excuse to bond with her. It is also unclear how much she actually enjoys her lessons, as she did start doing simpler designs to avoid the "self-punishment" of having to finish more complex designs.

Choice C is contradicted by the passage. The narrator's mom had high, not low, expectations for her work.

Choice D a minor detail. Yes, buckskin was used, as was an awl. But the main focus is on the process of beadwork,, not the nature of the materials.

Drill 1

The Redhawk Native American Arts Council is a nonprofit organization run by Native American artists and educators, people whose work often goes unnoticed by the general public. Its mission is to teach Native Americans and the public at large about Native American heritage through a variety of artistic mediums, including song, dance, theater, and visual arts. By contracting Native American artists to take part in educational programs, the organization helps artists be self-sufficient and connect with one another.

1. According to the text, one purpose of the Redhawk Native American Arts Council is to
   (A) offer vocational training for Native American children wishing to pursue artistic careers.
   (B) provide economic opportunities for an often overlooked group of artists.
   (C) encourage Native American artists to teach artists who are not Native American how to implement Native American stylistic elements in their works.
   (D) inform children about the general importance of art to cultures across the globe.

The following passage is adapted from the memoir *A Daughter of the Samurai* by Etsu Inagaki Sugimoto.

I was about eight years old when I had my first taste of meat. For twelve centuries, following the introduction of the Buddhist religion, which forbids the killing of animals, the Japanese people were vegetarians. In later years, however, both belief and custom have changed considerably, and now, though meat is not universally eaten, it can be found in all restaurants and hotels. But when I was a child it was looked upon with horror and loathing. My sister and I confided to each other that we liked the taste of meat. But neither of us mentioned this to anyone else; for we both loved Grandmother, and we knew our disloyalty would sadden her heart. The introduction of foreign food helped greatly to break down the wall of tradition which shut our people away from the world of the West, but sometimes the change was made at a great cost.

2. According to the text, the narrator's first experience with meat
   (A) aroused a moral conflict within the narrator.
   (B) permanently severed the narrator's connection with her ancestral routes.
   (C) resulted in tension between her and her grandmother.
   (D) was indicative of Japan's increasing divergence from the West.

The excerpt below is adapted from *A Little Princess* by Frances Hodgson Burnett.

Anyone who has been at school with a teller of stories knows what the wonder means—how he or she is followed about and besought in a whisper to relate romances; how groups gather round and hang on the outskirts of the favored party in the hope of being allowed to join in and listen. Sara not only could tell stories, but she adored telling them. When she sat or stood in the midst of a circle and began to invent wonderful things, her green eyes grew big and shining, her cheeks flushed, and, without knowing that she was doing it, she began to act and made what she told lovely or alarming by the raising or dropping of her voice, the bend and sway of her slim body, and the dramatic movement of her hands. She forgot that she was talking to listening children; she saw and lived with the fairy folk, or the kings and queens and beautiful ladies, whose adventures she was narrating. Sometimes when she had finished her story, she was quite out of breath with excitement, and would lay her hand on her thin, little, quick-rising chest, and half laugh as if at herself.

3. What is the main idea of the text?
    (A) Sara generally has difficulty distinguishing fact from fiction.
    (B) Sara's obsession with becoming popular inspires her to become a storyteller.
    (C) Sara feels very satisfied when she tells stories to her peers.
    (D) Sara is bored by the material she learns in school and creates her own stories to pass the time.

At a time when many Black artists were drawn to Social Realism—with its emphasis on pressing social and political issues— artist and art educator Hilda Rue Wilkinson Brown generally rejected a mimetic approach to art and instead embraced creative abstractions, her thick brushstrokes adding poignancy to her figurative paintings that depicted her community's landscapes and people. For example, her painting *University Neighborhood* portrays Brown's walking route to her job in abstract form, presenting the scene in geometric fragments. Her painting *Side Street* similarly depicts a real road without faithfully depicting its geographical features.

4. Which choice best states the main idea about Brown?
    (A) Brown was unsympathetic with the social concerns of artists who partook in the Social Realism movement, which is reflected in her teachings and artwork.
    (B) Brown adjusted her brushstrokes in her paintings depending on if the subject was a person or a landscape
    (C) Brown's approach to art did not prioritize literal accuracy in the subjects it depicted.
    (D) The subjects of Brown's art were rarely inspired by her surroundings in the real world.

The excerpt below is from *Don Quixote* by Miguel Cervantes.

Just as Don Quixote desired, he and Sancho Panza encountered many dangerous and unusual adventures in the days that followed; for so often did the knight mistake shepherds, holy men, and peasant girls for miscreant knights, evil enchanters, and ladies in distress, that he was continually involved in ridiculous quarrels and brawls. No matter how frantically Sancho urged him to see things as they really were, Don Quixote paid no attention to him. But although these absurd encounters were matters of great seriousness to the knight, many who witnessed them were delighted and amused. Gradually, his exploits became known all over the countryside, and there were few who had not heard of that flower of chivalry, Don Quixote de la Mancha.

  5. According to the text, which of the following is true of Don Quixote?
   (A) He became legendary for battling forces of evil.
   (B) He entertained many people whom he encountered in his adventures.
   (C) He reluctantly took part in adventures out of a sense of patriotic duty.
   (D) He resented Sancho Panza for not going along with his delusions.

The excerpt below is adapted from *Heart of Darkness* by Joseph Conrad.

"And this also," said Marlow suddenly, "has been one of the dark places of the earth."

He was the only man of us who still "followed the sea." The worst that could be said of him was that he did not represent his class. He was a seaman, but he was a wanderer, too, while most seamen lead, if one may so express it, a sedentary life. The yarns* of seamen have a direct simplicity, the whole meaning of which lies within the shell of a cracked nut. But Marlow was not typical (if his propensity to spin yarns be excepted), and to him the meaning of an episode was not inside like a kernel but outside, enveloping the tale which brought it out only as a glow brings out a haze, in the likeness of one of these misty halos that sometimes are made visible by the spectral illumination of moonshine.

*yarns: stories

  6. According to the text, the narrator indicates that which of the following is true about Marlow?

   (A) He is unable to cooperate with his colleagues.
   (B) He embraces a sedentary lifestyle.
   (C) His favorite activity is telling stories.
   (D) He is atypical from his fellow seamen.

While the exact function of tribal libraries varies across the United States, many of them serve as repositories for cultural information, serving to preserve a given tribe's heritage and traditional language. Beyond providing basic library services, they are valued as learning centers, museums, and connection points to governmental resources. Tribal libraries have adapted to the digital age by embracing technology that assists them in performing important functions. For example, some tribal libraries make use of digital technologies to create educational content and connect tribal members to employment opportunities.

7. What is the main idea of the text?

(A) Though the responsibilities of tribal libraries have changed over time, they are still important venues for preserving Native histories and culture.

(B) Although tribal libraries have many functions, the most important is acting as a repository of traditional languages.

(C) Technology has taken over many responsibilities of traditional tribal librarians.

(D) Tribal libraries have been educating children for centuries.

The excerpt below is from "To One Coming North" by Claude Mckay.

And when the fields and streets are covered white
  And the wind-worried void is chilly, raw,
Or underneath a spell of heat and light
  The cheerless frozen spots begin to thaw,

Like me you'll long for home, where birds' glad song
  Means flowering lanes and leas and spaces dry,
And tender thoughts and feelings fine and strong,
  Beneath a vivid silver-flecked blue sky.

But oh! more than the changeless southern isles,
  When Spring has shed upon the earth her charm,
You'll love the Northland wreathed in golden smiles
  By the miraculous sun turned glad and warm.

8. According to the text, the speaker
(A) appreciates how spring transforms the North.
(B) regrets moving to the North because of its chilly winters.
(C) values consistency in seasonal conditions.
(D) believes most people would benefit from moving North.

The excerpt below is adapted from *Sense and Sensibility* by Jane Austen.

Edward Ferrars was not recommended to their good opinion by any peculiar graces of person or address. He was not handsome, and his manners required intimacy to make them pleasing. He was too diffident to do justice to himself; but when his natural shyness was overcome, his behavior gave every indication of an open, affectionate heart. His understanding was good, and his education had given it solid improvement. But he was neither fitted by abilities nor disposition to answer the wishes of his mother and sister, who longed to see him distinguished—as—they hardly knew what. They wanted him to make a fine figure in the world in some manner or other. His mother wished to interest him in political concerns, to get him into parliament, or to see him connected with some of the great men of the day. Mrs. John Dashwood wished it likewise; but in the meanwhile, till one of these superior blessings could be attained, it would have quieted her ambition to see him driving a barouche. But Edward had no turn for great men or barouches. All his wishes centered in domestic comfort and the quiet of private life. Fortunately he had a younger brother who was more promising.

9. According to the text,

(A) Edward frequently quarreled with his family members over his lack of defined goals.

(B) Edward's shyness prevents him from being promoted in his chosen career.

(C) Edward's modest ambitions for his own life are at odds with his family's expectations for him.

(D) Edward only advocated for himself when it came to securing his domestic comfort.

Sub-Saharan Africa is home to the baobab tree, also known as the "tree of life," which grows from a single-stemmed tree into a more complex structure with multiple stems. Baobab trees perform key ecological functions, such as promoting nutrient recycling and carbon sequestration. Ecologists are concerned that many of these trees, which can live upwards of 3,000 years, have recently been dying prematurely at alarmingly high rates: climate change and human development have rendered much of the tree's environment uninhabitable. Animals that spread baobab seeds have also become endangered and gone extinct, preventing many new seedlings from growing. The Great Green Wall project is one attempt to save baobab trees by growing a protective wall around the continent to restore 1 million square kilometers of degraded land and combat desertification.

10. According to the text, why are some ecologists concerned about the baobab tree in sub-Saharan Africa?

(A) They no longer produce seedlings that are capable of producing young trees.

(B) Their environments are being harmed by encroaching walls.

(C) Adult baobab trees are dying before the end of their natural lifespans.

(D) Their ecosystems lack the ability to maintain trees with complex structures.

The excerpt below is from *O Pioneers!* by Willa Cather. John Bergson is Alexandra's father and works as a farmer. Lou and Oscar are John's sons.

He often called his daughter in to talk to her about this. Before Alexandra was twelve years old she had begun to be a help to him, and as she grew older he had come to depend more and more upon her resourcefulness and good judgment. His boys were willing enough to work, but when he talked with them they usually irritated him. It was Alexandra who read the papers and followed the markets, and who learned by the mistakes of their neighbors. It was Alexandra who could always tell about what it had cost to fatten each steer, and who could guess the weight of a hog before it went on the scales closer than John Bergson himself. Lou and Oscar were industrious, but he could never teach them to use their heads about their work.

11. According to the text, which of the following is true about Alexandra?

(A) She is remarkably insightful in agricultural matters.

(B) Her brothers are envious of the favorable treatment their father gives her.

(C) Her natural talents for her work compensate for her relatively mediocre work ethic.

(D) She does a moderately serviceable job keeping apprised of developments in her industry.

Setting ambitious goals that are impossible or nearly impossible to achieve can certainly have its psychological downsides. However, some psychologists argue that there is value in setting lofty, impractical goals. Setting one's aims high generally leads to greater achievement in the long-run. For example, if you are a track athlete who sets a goal to win a race after two months of practice, training as if you expect to win will likely lead you to run a faster time than if you had originally aimed for a more modest goal, such as not finishing in the bottom 20%. Thus, while setting ambitious goals can lead to increased disappointment, on balance, it seems to generally inspire us to achieve more, ultimately bolstering self-satisfaction.

12. Which choice best states the main idea of the text?

(A) Although the accelerated rate of improvement often associated with setting lofty goals can be thrilling, it is not sustainable for most people.

(B) Most psychologists have long supported amateur athletes setting unattainable goals.

(C) Creating ambitious goals for oneself that have virtually no chance at being achieved is the best way to improve one's skills and achieve more.

(D) Even though failing to achieve ambitious goals can be somewhat upsetting, setting high-minded goals tends to enhance one's level of personal achievement and sense of accomplishment.

Thyreophoran dinosaurs, a clade of armored dinosaurs including Ankylosauria and Stegosauria, were long believed to have lived in the northern continents since most of the fossil record comes from Jurassic North America and Europe. In 2022, Facundo Riguetti and colleagues reported the discovery of a fossil related to the thyreophoran *Scelidosaurus* from the early Late Cretaceous in the Patagonian region of South America. The newly discovered dinosaur, *Jakapil kaniukura*, bears several unusual anatomical traits not typical of late Cretaceous thyreophorans and is the first definitive thyreophoran species from this region. Unlike most thyreophorans, *Jakapil kaniukura* was a bipedal thyreophoran, as was *Scutellosaurus*.

13. According to the text, why was the discovery of *Jakapil kaniukura* significant?

(A) It suggested that *Jakapil kaniukura* was more closely related to *Scutellosaurus* than to *Sclediosaurus*.

(B) The discovery of the fossil suggested that the geographic range for thyreophoran dinosaurs during the early Late Cretaceous period was more widespread than previously known.

(C) The fossil helps establish a more accurate timeline for the evolution of thyreophoran dinosaurs into Ankylosauria and Stegosauria in South America.

(D) The fossil provided the first evidence that thyreophoran dinosaurs lived during the Cretaceous era.

The excerpt below is from *Sister Carrie* by Theodore Dreiser.

Caroline, or Sister Carrie, as she had been half affectionately termed by the family, was possessed of a mind rudimentary in its power of observation and analysis. Self-interest with her was high, but not strong. It was, nevertheless, her guiding characteristic. Warm with the fancies of youth, pretty with the insipid prettiness of the formative period, possessed of a figure promising eventual shapeliness and an eye alight with certain native intelligence, she was a fair example of the middle American class—two generations removed from the emigrant. Books were beyond her interest—knowledge a sealed book. In the intuitive graces she was still crude. She could scarcely toss her head gracefully. Her hands were almost ineffectual. The feet, though small, were set flatly. And yet she was interested in her charms, quick to understand the keener pleasures of life, ambitious to gain in material things. A half-equipped little knight she was, venturing to reconnoiter the mysterious city and dreaming wild dreams of some vague, far-off supremacy, which should make it prey and subject—the proper penitent, groveling at a woman's slipper.

14. According to the text, which of the following is true about Sister Carrie?

(A) She strongly desires acquiring tangible possessions.

(B) Family conflict prompts her to move to the city to improve her station in life.

(C) She wishes she had more interest in reading to amass her knowledge.

(D) Her favorite activity is enjoying pleasurable outings around the city.

The poem below is "I am Nobody! Who are You?" by Emily Dickinson.

I'm Nobody! Who are you?
Are you – Nobody – too?
Then there's a pair of us!
Don't tell! they'd advertise – you know!

How dreary – to be – Somebody!
How public – like a Frog –
To tell one's name – the livelong June –
To an admiring Bog!

15. Which of the following is one central idea of the text?
    (A) Fame requires that people engage in taxing self-promotion.
    (B) Being anonymous is generally preferable to being a public figure.
    (C) Maintaining a public persona precludes one from experiencing genuine companionship.
    (D) Privacy is underrated by most people in modern society.

The passage below is adapted from *Indian Boyhood* by Ohiyesa.

The Indian boy was a prince of the wilderness. He had but very little work to do during the period of his boyhood. His principal occupation was the practice of a few simple arts in warfare and the chase. Aside from this, he was master of his time. Whatever was required of us boys was quickly performed: then the field was clear for our games and plays. There was always keen competition among us. We felt very much as our fathers did in hunting and war—each one strove to excel all the others. Our sports were molded by the life and customs of our people; indeed, we practiced only what we expected to do when grown. Our games were feats with the bow and arrow, foot and pony races, wrestling, swimming and imitation of the customs and habits of our fathers. We had sham fights with mud balls and willow wands; we played lacrosse, made war upon bees, shot winter arrows (which were used only in that season), and coasted upon the ribs of animals and buffalo robes.

16. According to the narrator,
    (A) most Indian boys were overscheduled with a variety of tasks that would prepare them for their specialized adult occupations.
    (B) Indian boys were divided into teams based on preexisting family and community rivalries when playing sports.
    (C) sports served a pragmatic purpose in the Indian boy's life.
    (D) Indian boys were exposed to a variety of sports so that they would not grow bored.

In 1964, Peter Higgs proposed the existence of the Higgs Boson particle, a wave in a field believed to fill the universe and give mass to elementary particles. For many years, the existence of this particle remained mere conjecture. In 2012, however, a Large Hydrogen Collider (LHC) was used to prove Higgs's hypotheses correct. Surrounded by superconducting magnets, the LHC contains protons that stream at speeds approaching the speed of light, leading to millions of collisions, some of which would be expected to produce a Higgs particle. While Higgs particles form too quickly to be detected directly, scientists can predict which types of particles Higgs particles will decay into: the detection of these decay products ultimately led to the confirmation of their existence.

17. Which choice best states the main idea of the text?

    (A) It is difficult to detect the Higgs Boson particle because it can only exist intact momentarily.

    (B) Most scientists who propose controversial hypotheses are ultimately vindicated by empirical evidence.

    (C) Researchers proved the existence of the Higgs Boson particle years after it was initially proposed.

    (D) Magnets are the most important component of the technology needed to confirm the presence of subatomic particles.

The excerpt below is from "The Dubliners" by James Joyce.

He was called Little Chandler because, though he was but slightly under the average stature, he gave one the idea of being a little man. His hands were white and small, his frame was fragile, his voice was quiet and his manners were refined. He took the greatest care of his fair silken hair and moustache, and used perfume discreetly on his handkerchief. The half-moons of his nails were perfect, and when he smiled you caught a glimpse of a row of childish white teeth.

18. According to the passage, which of the following is true about Little Chandler?

    (A) He intimidates others with his refined appearance.

    (B) He is ashamed of his short stature.

    (C) He makes friends easily because of his gentle personality.

    (D) He puts significant effort into personal grooming.

The excerpt below is adapted from "A Blunder" by Anton Chekhov.

"Don't go on like that!" said Shchupkin, striking a match against his checked trousers. "I never wrote you any letters!"

"I like that! As though I didn't know your writing!" giggled the girl with an affected shriek, continually peeping at herself in the glass. "I knew it at once! And what a strange man you are! You are a writing master, and you write like a spider! How can you teach writing if you write so badly yourself?"

"H'm!...That means nothing. The great thing in writing lessons is not the hand one writes, but keeping the boys in order. You hit one on the head with a ruler, make another kneel down. Besides, there's nothing in handwriting! Nekrassov was an author, but his handwriting's a disgrace, there's a specimen of it in his collected works."

"You are not Nekrassov. (…)"

19. Based on the text, how does Shchupkin respond to the girl's question about his handwriting?

(A) He says the nature of his handwriting means nothing, even though he concedes many popular writers are more gifted than he is.

(B) He invokes the example of Nekrassov to support the point that strong writing and strong penmanship are incompatible aims.

(C) He counters that the quality of his penmanship should not be the basis on which to pass negative judgments about his writing capabilities.

(D) He expresses sympathy for the girl's perspective on one of his prominent flaws, even though the question clearly annoys him.

The excerpt below is adapted from *The Song of the Lark* by Willa Cather.

"I don't see how you stood it. I don't believe I could. I don't see how people can stand it to get knocked out, anyhow!" Thea spoke with such fierceness that Ray glanced at her in surprise.

"No occasion for you to see," he said warmly. "There'll always be plenty of other people to take the knocks for you."

"That's nonsense, Ray." Thea spoke impatiently and leaned lower still, frowning at the red star. "Everybody's up against it for himself, succeeds or fails—himself."

"In one way, yes," Ray admitted, knocking the sparks from his pipe out into the soft darkness that seemed to flow like a river beside the car. "But when you look at it another way, there are a lot of halfway people in this world who help the winners win, and the failers fail. If a man stumbles, there's plenty of people to push him down. But if he's like 'the youth who bore,' those same people are foreordained to help him along. They may hate to, worse than blazes, and they may do a lot of cussin' about it, but they have to help the winners and they can't dodge it. It's a natural law, like what keeps the big clock up there going, little wheels and big, and no mix-up."

20. Based on the text, Thea and Ray disagree about
    (A) whether it is worth being upset over the challenges one faces in life.
    (B) the extent to which one's life outcomes are shaped by the actions of others.
    (C) the moral responsibility people harbor in guiding those who are less fortunate.
    (D) which types of people are more deserving of experiencing professional success.

Researchers led by Forman Williams on the International Space Station (ISS) have discovered a type of cool burning flame that could prove useful in the creation of more fuel efficient vehicles. Such research can only be conducted in the microgravity environment of space. Although the cool flames result from chemical reactions similar to those on Earth, they can only exist for a short time on Earth. While the buoyancy on Earth causes fuel droplets to lose their symmetry, the lack of buoyancy in space allows them to retain their spherical shape and last long enough for scientists to measure for cool flames.

21. According to the text, studies on cool burning flames can't be conducted as effectively on Earth as on the International Space Station (ISS) because
    (A) gravity on Earth is much weaker than on the ISS.
    (B) the technology used to measure cool flames is too cumbersome to function on Earth.
    (C) the environments of Earth and the space station have different levels of buoyancy.
    (D) the underlying chemical reactions producing the cool flames cannot occur on Earth.

The poem below is "'Hope" is the Thing With Feathers" by Emily Dickinson.

"Hope" is the thing with feathers -
That perches in the soul -
And sings the tune without the words -
And never stops - at all -

And sweetest - in the Gale - is heard -
And sore must be the storm -
That could abash the little Bird
That kept so many warm -

I've heard it in the chillest land -
And on the strangest Sea -
Yet - never - in Extremity,
It asked a crumb - of me.

22. Based on the text, in what way is hope like a bird?
    (A) It is formidable in the face of challenging circumstances.
    (B) It loses its power with the passage of time.
    (C) It is dependent on outside forces for nourishment.
    (D) It draws strength from inclement weather.

The passage below is adapted from *White Fang* by Jack London. White Fang is a wolfdog and Weedon Scott is his new owner.

He learned to adjust himself in many ways to his new mode of life. It was borne in upon him that he must let his master's dogs alone. Yet his dominant nature asserted itself, and he had first to thrash them into an acknowledgment of his superiority and leadership. This accomplished, he had little trouble with them. They gave trail to him when he came and went or walked among them, and when he asserted his will they obeyed. In the same way, he came to tolerate Matt—as a possession of his master. His master rarely fed him. Matt did that, it was his business; yet White Fang divined that it was his master's food he ate and that it was his master who thus fed him vicariously. It was Matt who tried to put him into the harness and make him haul sleds with the other dogs. But Matt failed. It was not until Weedon Scott put the harness on White Fang and worked him, that he understood. He took it as his master's will that Matt should drive him and work him just as he drove and worked his master's other dogs.

23. What is the main idea of the text?

    (A) White Fang becomes less skeptical of other dogs and Matt once he learns that his master treasures White Fang above all others.

    (B) White Fang gradually develops admiration for Matt and his master's other dogs.

    (C) White Fang does his best to avoid interacting with all living beings besides his master.

    (D) White Fang puts the interests of his master ahead of all others.

The excerpt below is adapted from *The Song of the Lark* by Willa Cather.

Thea, however, had one in the person of her addle-pated aunt, Tillie Kronborg. Tillie's mind was a curious machine; when she was awake it went round like a wheel when the belt has slipped off, and when she was asleep she dreamed follies. But she had intuitions. She knew, for instance, that Thea was different from the other Kronborgs, worthy though they all were. Her romantic imagination found possibilities in her niece. When she was sweeping or ironing, or turning the ice-cream freezer at a furious rate, she often built up brilliant futures for Thea, adapting freely the latest novel she had read.

24. What is the main idea of the text?

(A) Tillie holds Thea in high esteem.

(B) Tillie believes Thea is the only Kronborg who will ever amount to anything.

(C) Thea revels in the attention Tillie gives her.

(D) Tillie often confuses details that happened in Thea's life with those that happened in the lives of characters in novels Tillie has read.

It has long been known that infants will play with objects they witnessed behave unexpectedly. It turns out, intentionally surprising infants might also improve learning outcomes. In one study, some infants were shown an expected event (a ball being stopped by a wall), and others were shown an unexpected event (the ball seeming to pass through the wall). All infants were taught that the ball squeaks. To ensure infants learned this information, the researchers moved the ball and a control object while a squeak played from a central location. The surprised infants spent more time looking at the ball. When a sound the infants did not hear was played (a rattling sound), infants in the surprised and expected conditions reacted similarly. This was evidence that surprised infants learned the original squeaking sound more effectively, on average.

25. According to the text, how did the researchers assess if the infants actually learned the ball made a squeak?

(A) By examining the amount of time infants gazed at the ball when the squeaking sound was played.

(B) By recording the amount of time infants spent playing with the ball and the control object.

(C) By studying how infants interacted with the researchers when different sounds were played.

(D) By asking the infants to either verbalize the name of the object that squeaked or point to it.

The poem below is adapted from William Shakespeare's "Sonnet 30." The poem is addressed to a friend.

> When to the sessions of sweet silent thought
> I summon up remembrance of things past,
> I sigh the lack of many a thing I sought,
> And with old woes new wail my dear time's waste:
>
> Then can I grieve at grievances foregone,
> And heavily from woe to woe tell o'er
>
> But if the while I think on thee, dear friend,
> All losses are restored and sorrows end.

26. What is the main idea of the text?
    (A) The narrator thanks the friend for the emotional labor he has endured in comforting him through a difficult time.
    (B) The narrator takes comfort in thinking about his friend while dwelling on past losses.
    (C) The narrator is reflecting on past disappointments in silence while actively planning a reunion to meet his friend.
    (D) The narrator is too overcome by grief to continue conversing with his friend.

Pre-Lesson Reflection Activity

Consider the following claims and ask yourself the following questions.

1) *Intuitively, to what extent does each claim seem reasonable to you?*
2) *What sort of additional information might make each claim more or less convincing?*
3) *To what extent is each claim open to legitimate disagreements by people who have all the relevant information needed to make an assessment?*

Claim 1: Ancient human farmers who moved from the Near East to Europe during the Neolithic Revolution brought their dogs with them rather than simply adopt local European dogs.

Claim 2: Listening to happy music makes people more creative.

Claim 3: The government should invest in advanced technologies that will increase productivity, even if that means millions of workers will lose jobs.

Each of these claims is very different in nature.

Claim 1 is a falsifiable statement. Either farmers did bring their dogs or they did not. There is no gray area. This claim probably seems like it *could* be true to you, but of course you would need more information. Maybe DNA evidence of ancient dogs found among the settlers' farms can reveal if these dogs had notable genetic differences from local dogs. Perhaps written records might indicate if dogs were brought along migration routes. Overall, this claim is open to disagreement in the absence of complete information, but with complete information, we can verify if this is right or wrong.

Claim 2 also might sound reasonable to you. Maybe you know from experience that listening to happy music helps you be more creative when working on projects. Experimental data might help verify whether your intuitions are correct. Perhaps if controlled experiments were done that showed people listening to happy music generated more creative ideas than a similar group of people listening to no music or sad music, this claim would be better supported. Still, it's possible this claim can be subject to disagreement among experts if different experiments reach different conclusions. Maybe flaws in the study design made it look like happy music had a positive effect on creativity when another factor was more relevant.

Claim 3 is probably the least "provable" and most controversial. It is more a statement one can agree or disagree with as opposed to a factual statement whose accuracy can be verified. You would likely want to hear about the pros and cons of such a policy from research, balance them against each other, and come to your own conclusion. For example, if you were to learn that there was a viable strategy to help the people losing their jobs (e.g., funding assistance for training in related careers), you might be more inclined to support this policy. If you learned that this policy is projected to cause personal problems for millions of people while doing little to help the lives of average people, you might be more inclined to oppose it.

Hopefully this exercise was helpful in getting you to think about the power of evidence in supporting claims. **Command of Evidence** questions in some ways are the mirror opposite of **Main Idea** questions. As we saw in lesson 1, to determine the main idea we had to integrate various pieces of information or evidence to determine the broad idea or claim they supported. In **Command of Evidence** questions, by contrast, you will often be given a main idea or claim and asked to find information that supports or does not support that idea. These questions might have you work with information from a text or a graph, generally a bar graph or a data table. Below we will examine some of the common types of **Command of Evidence** questions.

Question Type 1: Selecting a quote that supports a point.
Some questions will briefly tell you a main idea or claim and ask you to pick a quote that provides evidence for it. For that reason, let's take a step back and review the components of an argument.

Arguments have three components: claims, reasoning, and evidence.
1) A **claim** is an assertion that something is true. A **thesis statement** is often used to present the central claim of an argumentative essay.
   - *People should exercise regularly.*
   - *Teachers should make use of neuroscience principles in the classroom.*
   - *Mass production can cause problems for companies.*

2) **Reasoning** is rationale or reasons for supporting the author's claim. Authors must provide a logical explanation for WHY their point of view makes sense.
   - *Exercising helps people stay healthy.*
   - *Teachers who have a better understanding of how the brain works can better adapt their lessons to their students' needs.*
   - *Mass production makes it difficult to alter the design of a product once production has started. Because all products produced are the same, customers' diverse preferences might not be met.*

3) **Evidence** includes examples, facts, statistics, anecdotes, or studies that support an argument. Writers must provide supportive examples that SHOW that the claim is or could be true. Reasoning without evidence is NOT sufficient to prove a claim.
   - *People who do not exercise experience higher rates of obesity and heart disease than those who exercise for at least four hours a week.*
   - *Researchers found that students in classrooms whose teachers made use of educational neuroscience principles performed better on an exam than students in a control group whose teacher taught the same unit without employing such principles.*
   - *The Ford Model T was produced efficiently by mass production. It lost market share to General Motors, which offered more customized cars that appealed to a more diverse consumer base.*

Suppose an SAT question asked you to find a quote that supports the idea that a certain pollutant threatens the health of rivers. A correct answer might cite a study showing specific damage that pollutant did to a river (e.g., such as by changing pH levels in a way that harms fish). If a question asked you for evidence that supports a claim that a character feels remorseful, you might look for a quote in which a character expresses guilt for the pain their actions have caused.

To approach quote selection questions, do the following:
1) Read the question carefully to determine the main point that needs support.
2) In your own words, briefly consider the type of evidence that would make this claim/idea true.
3) Examine each choice carefully. Eliminate any that either contradict the point being made or that do not support the main point one way or the other.

Sample 1

In Jane Austen's *Emma,* Emma Woodhouse is portrayed as somewhat of a busybody who interferes in the lives of those around her. Which of the following quotations best illustrates this claim?

A) "Emma Woodhouse, handsome, clever, and rich, with a comfortable home and happy disposition, seemed to unite some of the best blessings of existence; and had lived nearly twenty-one years in the world with very little to distress or vex her."

B) "The real evils, indeed, of Emma's situation were the power of having rather too much her own way, and a disposition to think a little too well of herself; these were the disadvantages which threatened alloy to her many enjoyments."

C) "She was the youngest of the two daughters of a most affectionate, indulgent father; and had, in consequence of her sister's marriage, been mistress of his house from a very early period."

D) "With insufferable vanity had she believed herself in the secret of everybody's feelings; with unpardonable arrogance proposed to arrange everybody's destiny. She was proved to have been universally mistaken; and she had not quite done nothing–for she had done mischief."

We are looking for evidence that Emma is a busybody, someone who frequently meddles in the lives of other people. We might predict that the right answer choice will give a specific example of her interfering in others' lives or a reference to her general tendency to not mind her own business.

Choice A just talks about Emma's happy upbringing. There is no indication about her tendency to interfere in others' affairs.

Choice B seems better than A, as it does mention a negative quality in Emma, namely that she thinks highly of herself. This could lead her to overestimate her capabilities and interfere in others' lives with advice, but this seems like a bit of a stretch of an inference to make. We will keep this choice in contention for now, but it is probably wrong.

Choice C seems wrong. We get the sense that Emma is spoiled by her father, but we don't learn about the effect of this on her personality. Either B or D will be right.

Choice D is best. Not only is Emma a bit delusional about her capabilities, but she also tries to "arrange everybody's destiny." In other words, she tries to dictate aspects of their life paths. She accomplished nothing but mischief, showing her attempts to help others have backfired. Choice **D is correct.**

Question Type 2: Evaluating Claims/Hypotheses (Text)

In the beginning of this lesson, we learned about **claims**. Other questions on the SAT will ask you about hypotheses. A **hypothesis** is a proposed explanation for a phenomenon. We make hypotheses all the time in our daily lives. For example, when your favorite artist announces that he will be releasing a new album, you might hypothesize how many people will buy it or what types of songs might be included. If you drink coffee at night shortly before going to bed, you might hypothesize how doing so will affect you. Will you be unable to fall asleep as quickly as usual? If so, will that affect your ability to focus on an important task the next day, such as an exam or a game?

In research, scientists make hypotheses to explain phenomena in fields ranging from the natural sciences (such as hypotheses about factors that influence the health of ecosystems or conditions needed to support life on other planets) to the humanities (such as hypotheses about the true authorship of ancient texts or about the secret meaning behind a mysterious painting), to the social sciences (such as hypotheses about how peer pressure will alter behavior in morally fraught situations or about how subliminal messaging in advertisements affects purchasing behavior).

Below are some examples of hypotheses. Most hypotheses on the SAT generally fall into two categories, which we will informally call **historical hypotheses** and **cause and effect hypotheses**.

Historical hypotheses typically try to explain events that happened in the distant past.
1) **Historical hypothesis:** Wolves did not domesticate themselves; rather humans collected, adopted, and artificially selected for the tamest wolf pups to domesticate them into what are now modern dogs.

This is an example of a hypothesis that tries to explain a past event. Genetic, archaeological, and animal behavior research might indicate how likely this hypothesis is to be correct.

- **Historical hypothesis:** While Homer's *Iliad* included some legendary material, the events described were largely historical.

This is an example of a historical hypothesis that contends a certain set of events described in a work actually happened. There is currently scholarly debate on this. Archaeological finds or written records about events that seem to parallel those described in the *Iliad* would strengthen this hypothesis.

Cause and effect hypotheses tend to deal with scientific, psychological, and sociological phenomena occurring today.
1) **Cause and Effect Hypothesis:** Doing crossword puzzles improves English vocabulary in 8th grade second language learners.
2) **Cause and Effect Hypothesis:** Pesticide use has no effect on the pollen output of common ragweed.

Depending on the issue at hand, a **controlled experiment** can be used to test some of these hypotheses. In a controlled experiment, subjects are divided into two or more groups. One group (the **control group**) does not get exposure to the "treatment," or the variable of interest (the thing you think is causing something else to happen). The **experimental group** (also known as the treatment group) does receive the variable of interest.

In the case of the first hypothesis, the "treatment" would be access to crossword puzzles. To test this hypothesis, you might give two comparable groups of students a pre-test on vocabulary followed by vocabulary instruction. However, only the treatment group would perform crossword puzzles while the control group would not. At the end of the study, you can give both groups a vocabulary test and see if the experimental group improved significantly more than the control group did. If the experimental group improved more, this finding would provide support for the hypothesis.

To test the second hypothesis, you might grow two plots of ragweed in identical conditions but only give the experimental group pesticide. After a few weeks of monitoring plants in both groups, you can examine if the pollen content differed meaningfully between the control and experimental groups. If there is no significant difference, this finding would support the hypothesis.

On some SAT questions, you will be asked to determine which information will strengthen a claim or hypothesis.

To answer evidence strengthening questions, do the following:
1) Make sure you understand the claim or hypothesis fully by reading the passage carefully.
2) Predict in your own words what type of information might make the claim/hypothesis seem more convincing to you.
3) Systematically go through each choice. Eliminate choices that seem to contradict the claim/hypothesis or any that neither strengthen nor weaken it.

Sample 2

Krysle E. Zunigia and colleagues were interested in determining if exercise can improve memory. In an experiment, college students in the exercise condition were instructed to perform exercise over three days while students in the sedentary condition were instructed not to exercise. Subjects were exposed to a series of cognitive tests at the start of the study (before the exercise group did their exercises) and again at the end of the study. The researchers hypothesized that students who exercised would see larger improvements in memory than students who were sedentary.

Which of the following, if true, would most strongly support Zunigia's hypothesis?
   A) Students in the sedentary condition improved their scores on a free recall test by a significantly greater percentage than did those in the exercise condition.
   B) Students in the sedentary condition did not see improvements on a task of metacognitive accuracy.
   C) Students in the exercise condition improved their scores on a free recall test by a significantly greater percentage than did those in the sedentary condition.
   D) Students in the exercise condition lost more weight during the study period, on average, then did participants in the sedentary condition.

The hypothesis is that exercise improves memory. The right answer should probably give specific evidence of this: namely, subjects in the exercise condition saw enhanced improvements in memory relative to the sedentary group.

Choice A contradicts the hypothesis and would actually weaken it.

Choice B does not address the hypothesis (the choice deals with metacognitive accuracy rather than memory). It also makes no comparison between the groups.

Choice C is correct. If the exercise group improved more in a test of memory than did the sedentary group, this would support the hypothesis.

Choice D is irrelevant to the research question, so it does not help or undermine the hypothesis.

Other SAT questions, you will be asked to determine which information will **weaken** a claim or hypothesis.

To answer evidence weakening questions, do the following:
1) Make sure you understand the claim or hypothesis fully by reading the passage carefully.
2) Predict in your own words what type of information might make the claim/hypothesis seem LESS convincing to you.
3) Systematically go through each choice. Eliminate any that seem to SUPPORT the claim/hypothesis or any that neither strengthen nor weaken it.

Sample 3

Classical physicists define vacuums as regions of empty space lacking real particles, which are detectable particles such as electrons and positrons. It is generally thought that adding a real particle to a vacuum should raise its energy level, but some theorists suggest that adding such a particle can actually decrease its energy, creating real particles. A quantum physicist asserts that in order for a vacuum to decay, a necessary precondition is an intense electric field, charging the vacuum. Such a field can move a vacuum into a state of lower energy in which it is unstable enough for it to decay when real particles form in its region of space. But only a superheavy atomic nucleus in the immediate vicinity of a vacuum could be strong enough to produce such a field.

Which of the following, if true, would most seriously weaken the quantum physicist's assertion?
A) Scientists placed a superheavy nucleus far away from a vacuum, but the vacuum fails to develop an electric charge.
B) Scientists produced an intense electric field close to a vacuum, and a positron and electron spontaneously formed in the vacuum's region of space.
C) Scientists placed a superheavy nucleus near a vacuum, but no real particles form in its region of space.
D) Scientists introduced electrons and positrons into a vacuum, but the stability of the vacuum remains unchanged.

The main assertion is that a vacuum can be decayed by a superheavy atomic nucleus placed right near a vacuum. This would produce an intense enough electric charge to destabilize the vacuum and result in real particles being formed. We are looking for a choice that suggests this is not true.

Choice A does not seriously undermine the assertion. The physicist stated that the superheavy nucleus must be placed in "the immediate vicinity" of the vacuum in order for the vacuum to become charged. If the superheavy nucleus were placed far away, the physicist would likely expect the vacuum not to become charged.

Choice B would actually strengthen the assertion. Positrons and electrons are real particles. If they formed in the region of space after a superheavy nucleus were placed near a vacuum, this would show the assertion is correct.

Choice C is correct. If no real particles formed when the superheavy nucleus is placed near the vacuum, this could suggest the assertion is wrong, as the prediction failed to come true.

Choice D is not relevant to the main argument, which argues that only a superheavy nucleus can produce an electric field strong enough to affect the stability of a vacuum. The fact that adding a different type of particle in a vacuum did not change its stability would not challenge the physicist's assertion.

Question Type 3: Evaluating Claims/Hypotheses (Graphs)

Some questions on the SAT will have you evaluate support for claims based on graphs accompanying texts. Approach these questions in much the same way as you would text-based evidence questions, but keep the following points in mind.

1) Some choices will provide information that is an incorrect reading of information in the graph. These choices can be easily eliminated for failing to provide accurate data.
2) Of the choices that do provide accurate data, some choices will provide information that is not relevant to the original question. Make sure you are clear about what the question is asking.

Suppose a state was conducting a study on student feelings of engagement (involvement) in school communities over the course of several years. As part of the study, students in several schools rate their feelings of engagement on a scale of 1 to 5, such that "1" means a student does not feel very engaged in the school community, and "5" means a student does feel very engaged. The results for the mean levels of self-reported school engagement for four schools are shown below. **Think about the trends you observe both within and between schools with regards to school engagement levels.**

School	2016	2018	2020	2022
A	3.4	3.1	3.1	2.8
B	3.5	3.3	2.8	2.4
C	3.1	3.0	2.7	2.1
D	3.2	3.3	3.7	4.3

Suppose you wanted to use this table to argue that school engagement was decreasing for most schools in the sample. In that case, since you are making an argument about **change over time,** you would need to cite data over **multiple years**. The fact that schools A, B, and C saw decreases between 2016 and 2022 would be good evidence to support this point. Just giving data about 2022 would not itself be enough to support this idea.

Suppose you wanted to argue that the trend of school engagement levels in school D was different from this trend in school C despite both schools having similar starting levels of engagement. In this case, you would need to cite data from school C and D in 2016 (to show that their reported engagement levels were very similar initially) as well as data from a later year, preferably 2020 or 2022.

Most graph-based questions will have you find information that supports a claim using data in a table or graph.

To answer graph questions about data that support a claim, do the following:
1) Read the paragraph and identify the claim being made.
2) Predict what type of data would best support this claim.
3) Eliminate any choices that provide inaccurate information (if any).
4) Of the accurate choices, determine which one is most relevant to advancing the claim.

Sample 4

	Percentage of Respondents with Confidence in Institutions (2022)		
	Quite a lot to a Great Deal	Some	None to Very Little
Medical System	38	38	24
Congress	7	36	57
Television News	11	35	53
Big Business	14	43	41
Small Business	68	25	6

Gallup regularly conducts surveys of Americans on a variety of issues. In one such survey, Gallup asks respondents to indicate how confident on a scale of "none" (lowest possible rating) to "a great deal" (highest possible rating) they feel about various political, social, and economic institutions. Data for five of these institutions are shown in the table above. A student concludes that the data indicate Americans' confidence in institutions varies widely by institution type. For example, _____.

Which of the following best describes data from the table to support the claim?
A) only 7% of respondents have at least quite a lot of confidence in Congress, while 57% have very little to no confidence in it.
B) 35% of respondents report having some confidence in television news, and 38% report having some confidence in the medical system.
C) 53% of respondents have no to very little confidence in the medical system, while 41% of respondents have no to very little confidence in small business.
D) 68% of respondents report having quite a lot to a great deal of trust in small business, while 14% report having the same level of confidence in big business.

The right answer needs to meet three criteria:
  1) accurately report on data from the table.
  2) compare data between two institutions.
  3) show a meaningful difference between the two institutions.

Choice C uses data inaccurately. In actuality, 24% of respondents have no to very little confidence in the medical system, while 6% of respondents have no to very little confidence in small business. We can eliminate this choice quickly.

Choice A gives an accurate summary of the data, but it only discusses one institution (Congress). Thus, while this data is accurate, it is not relevant to the main point that confidence levels vary between institutions.

Choice B does accurately compare data between the medical system and television. However, the percentages are very close (only 3 percentage points apart). It might weakly support the argument since these percentages are not identical, but there might be a better option.

 Choice D is correct. Like B, it shows an accurate difference in confidence levels between two institutions, but this difference is very dramatic (54 percentage points). It would provide the strongest support for the claim.

If you are asked to find data that best undermines, or weakens, a claim, search for an answer that shows data *inconsistent* with the researcher's prediction. This is similar to how we approached text-based command of evidence questions in which arguments were undermined.

To answer graph questions about data that weaken a claim, do the following:
1) Read the paragraph and identify the claim being made. 2) Predict what type of data would WEAKEN this claim. 3) Eliminate any choices that provide inaccurate information (if any). 4) Of the accurate choices, determine which one is most relevant to <u>weakening</u> the claim.

Sample 5

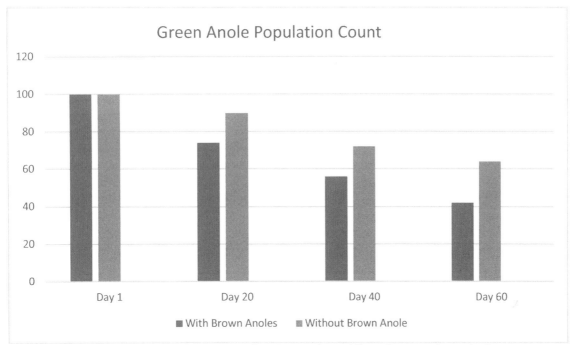

After reading an article that brown anoles (a species of lizard) sometimes bully or eat green anoles (another lizard species), a biology student decided to investigate the effect of brown anoles on green anoles. He placed two groups of green anoles into enclosures, one with and one without brown anoles and counted the population of green anoles for 60 days. The student concluded that the reduction in the green anole population count was fully attributable to the presence of brown anoles.

Which choice best describes data from the graph that weaken the student's conclusion?
A) Both enclosures saw noteworthy decreases in green anole numbers.
B) The green anole count was the same in both enclosures on day 1.
C) Green anoles decreased more in the enclosure with brown anoles.
D) The largest decline in the green anole population for those in the enclosure with brown anoles occurred between days 1 and 20.

The student expects the population in the green anoles to decline entirely because of the brown anole population. If this were true, we would expect little to no decrease in the green anole population in the enclosure without brown anoles and substantial reductions in the enclosure with brown anoles. Evidence that green anole population declines significantly even when brown anoles are absent would weaken this conclusion.

Choice A looks good. We do see that enclosures with and without brown anoles saw notable decreases in the green anole population. Therefore, the presence of brown anoles can't fully explain the decline, though it likely accelerated this decline. **Choice A is correct**.

Choice B is a true statement but it has no bearing on the conclusion. We only care about the change in the green anole population over time. Just knowing the initial value is not relevant to the conclusion.

Choice C is a true statement, but it does not support the conclusion that the decline in the green anole population was ENTIRELY due to brown anoles. The fact that both enclosures showed declines weakens the conclusion. At best, C shows brown anoles might accelerate the decline, but other factors are at play.

Choice D is true but irrelevant. It makes no mention of data from the enclosure lacking brown anoles, which is essential to supporting the student's conclusion. Again, the fact that both enclosures showed reductions means other factors contributed to the green anole population change besides the presence of brown anoles.

Drill 2

In the poem "Sometimes " by Maggie Pogue Johnson, she indicates that many people choose not to maximize the good that they are capable of doing in the world, writing, _____.

1. Which quotation from "Sometimes" most effectively illustrates this claim?
   - (A) "Sometimes the days seem dark and dreary/We wonder what is life;
       Sometimes of work we soon grow weary/ All pleasures seem but strife."
   - (B) "Sometimes if we'd stop to think/And count the good deeds we do/
       To help those on Poverty's brink/We'd find them to be few."
   - (C) "Sometimes 'twould help us to resolve/That each day while we live,/
       Some difficult problem we will solve/Or aid to others give."
   - (D) "By our actions, by the deeds we do,/Each day while we live,/Let them be many,
       or let them be few,/We make life what it is."

A student tested his hypothesis that *Papaver nudicaule* (more commonly known as the Iceland poppy) grows best in alkaline (or less acidic) environments. To test this hypothesis, he placed 20 seedlings of *Papaver nudicaule* in soil that had lime added to it, as lime is known to make soil more alkaline. He put another 20 seedlings in soil without lime as a control condition. The groups were otherwise exposed to identical growing conditions, and their growth was monitored for three weeks.

2. Which of the following, if true, would most directly weaken the student's hypothesis?
   (A) The mass of the poppies in the group grown with lime in its soil was significantly greater than the mass of the poppies in the group grown without lime in its soil at the end of the three weeks.
   (B) The poppies planted in the soil without lime grew significantly taller than the poppies planted in the soil with lime at the end of the experiment.
   (C) The seeds for the poppies planted in soil without line sprouted significantly later than did those in the soil with lime.
   (D) Significantly more seedlings sprouted in the group grown with lime than sprouted in the group grown without lime.

City Residents Supporting Funding for a Dog Park

District	Percent Supporting Policy
1	56%
2	87%
3	42%
4	25%

A researcher was comparing support for funding for a new dog park among residents in four districts of a large city, finding that support varied widely between districts. The researcher found the lowest level of support for the dog park in any region was 25%, which is seen in_____

3. Which of the following best uses data from the chart to complete the text?
   (A) District 1.
   (B) District 2.
   (C) District 3.
   (D) District 4.

City	January Average Low Daily Temperature (degrees Fahrenheit)	January Average High Daily Temperature (degrees Fahrenheit)
New York City, NY	28°	40°
Los Angeles, CA	49°	68°
Chicago, IL	20°	33°
Houston, TX	46°	64°

A student was interested in studying how much the weather affects where people live. She compared the average high and low temperatures in January for the four largest cities by population in the United States and noticed that temperatures varied widely depending on where people lived. For example, in January _____

4. Which choice uses data from the chart to best complete the text?
   (A) the average low temperature was 28 degrees for New York, while its average high temperature was 40 degrees.
   (B) the average high temperature was 68 degrees for Los Angeles and 64 degrees for Houston.
   (C) the average low temperature was 20 degrees for Chicago and 49 degrees for Los Angeles.
   (D) the average low temperature was 49 degrees for Los Angeles, while its average high temperature was 68 degrees.

In Kahlil Gibran's poem "On Friendship," he presents the claim that friendship can be a solution to one's problems.

5. Which quotation from "On Friendship" best illustrates this claim?
   (A) "When your friend speaks his mind you fear not the "nay" in your own mind/nor do you withhold the 'ay.'"
   (B) "Your friend is your needs answered/He is your field which you sow with love and reap with thanksgiving."
   (C) "For love that seeks aught but the disclosure of its own mystery us not love/ but a net cast forth: and only the unprofitable is caught."
   (D) "For that which you love most in him may be clearer in his absence, as the/ mountain to the climber is clearer from the plain."

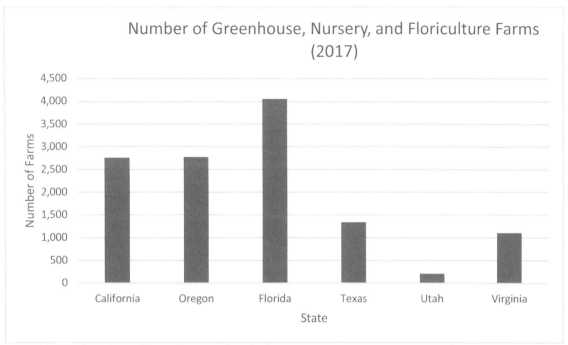

Number of Greenhouse, Nursery, and Floriculture Farms (2017)

Data Adapted from 2017 USDA Census of Agriculture

The greenhouse, nursery, and floriculture industry consists of establishments that grow any crop under covered conditions (such as inside greenhouses) and establishments that grow nursery stock and flower products, including shrubs, Christmas trees, and even some foods like tomatoes. The value of this industry is expected to grow by about 4% between 2021 and 2027 and includes over 9,550 producers generating revenues over $10 billion. This industry is growing more popular. According to the 2017 census, Florida had between 4,000 and 4,200 farms in the greenhouse, nursery, and floriculture industry, and _____

6. Which choice most effectively uses data from the table to complete the text?

(A) California and Texas each had between 2,500 and 3,000 farms in this industry.

(B) Texas had fewer than 900 farms in this industry.

(C) Oregon had between 2,000 and 3,000 farms in this industry.

(D) Virginia had under 1,000 farms in this industry.

A team of scientists examined the bones of wolves and dogs from 7,000 to 8,000 years ago. They found evidence that dogs had smaller frames, meaning they were unlikely to be able to hunt large prey. Wolves, by contrast, were capable of hunting prey much bigger than themselves, such as deer. Modern dogs have more copies of the AMY2B genes than wolves do, allowing them to digest starches common in human diets. Taken together, the evidence led the researchers to conclude that ancient dogs were reliant on humans for nutrition, while ancient wolves obtained their own food.

7. Which finding, if true, would best support the researchers' conclusion?
   (A) An analysis of the bones of ancient dogs showed that they consumed marine animals that they likely would not have been able to hunt themselves.
   (B) Humans have varying levels of the AMY2B gene related to the type of agriculture grown by their ancestors.
   (C) The dietary needs of wolves are stricter than those of dogs.
   (D) An investigation of collagen proteins in the bones of ancient dogs revealed that they consumed small amounts of deer.

The Fission Theory of the moon's origin held that the Earth was once rotating much faster than it is now, leading material from the Earth's crust and mantle—but not the Earth's much denser core—to be launched into space, forming the moon. The likely site of where the moon originated under this theory is the Pacific Ocean basin. Similarity between moon rocks and Earth rocks compositions has been cited as evidence for this theory.

8. Which of the following, if true, most seriously weakens the Fission Theory?
   (A) The relative abundances of oxygen isotopes of rocks on the lunar surface resemble those of rocks on Earth.
   (B) The density of the moon is lower than that of the Earth.
   (C) The concentration of iron on the moon is lower than on Earth.
   (D) The oxygen isotope compositions for volcanic glass and basalts deep below the lunar surface are distinct from those of Earth rocks.

There is great debate over the significance of the Olmec Civilization, which occupied parts of modern-day Mexico from approximately 1600–400 C.E. Some scholars, such as Jeffrey Blomster, consider the Olmec Civilization to be the mother of all other Mesoamerican cultures, such as the Maya and Aztecs, spreading its culture to other societies. For example, the Mesoamerican ballgame, which originated with the Olmecs, spread to nearly every other Mesoamerican culture. Other scholars, such as Takeshi Inomata, argue that the Olmec civilization was not a "mother" to other societies. Rather, different societies made their own unique cultural contributions and in turn influenced one another through interactions.

9. Which finding, if true, would most directly support Inomata's argument?
   (A) Artistic subjects, such as plumed serpents, appeared in Olmec art before appearing in the artwork of other Mesoamerican cultures.
   (B) Much of the religious imagery in Mesoamerican societies was similar from region to region.
   (C) Ceremonial architecture at a Mayan site in Ceibal predates the earliest ceremonial site in Olmec territory by about 200 years.
   (D) 725 pieces of pottery with Olmec designs throughout Central America had compositions of local Olmec ceramic and clays.

In "A Plea for Free Speech in Boston," Frederick Douglass discusses the importance of protecting free speech after a mob attacked a meeting assembled to discuss how to abolish slavery. His speech's central claim was that the right of free speech is not contingent on one's life circumstances:_____

10. Which quotation from the speech "A Plea for Free Speech in Boston" most effectively illustrates this claim?

(A) "The principles of human liberty, even if correctly apprehended, find but limited support in this hour of trial."

(B) "No right was deemed by the fathers of the Government more sacred than the right of speech."

(C) "To suppress free speech is a double wrong. It violates the rights of the hearer as well as those of the speaker."

(D) "A man's right to speak does not depend upon where he was born or upon his color. The simple quality of manhood is the solid basis of the right – and there let it rest forever."

Ablation Rate of Different Elements in Different Types of Cosmic Dust

Element	JFC	AST	HTC	OOC
Sodium	28%	75%	99%	100%
Silicon	6%	17%	87%	97%
Magnesium	5%	11%	85%	97%

Adapted from Carrillo-Sánchez JD, Nesvorný D, Pokorný P, Janches D, Plane JM. Sources of cosmic dust in the Earth's atmosphere. Geophys Res Lett. 2016 Dec 16;43(23):11979-11986. doi: 10.1002/2016GL071697. Epub 2016 Dec 14. PMID: 28275286; PMCID: PMC5319002.

There are several sources of dust in the cosmos: Jupiter family comet asteroids (JFC), Halley type comets (HTC), Oort cloud comets (OOC), and asteroid belt particles (AST). Researcher Juan Carrillo Sanchez found that the ablation rate (the rate at which dust vaporizes) for any given element is higher in faster-moving OOC and HTC dust than in slower-moving JFC and AST dust. For instance, while the ablation rate for silicon is 6% in JFC dust, the ablation rate for

11. Which choice most effectively uses data from the table to complete the text?

(A) silicon is 17% in AST dust.

(B) sodium is 28% in JFC dust.

(C) silicon is 97% in OOC dust.

(D) magnesium is 85% in HTC dust.

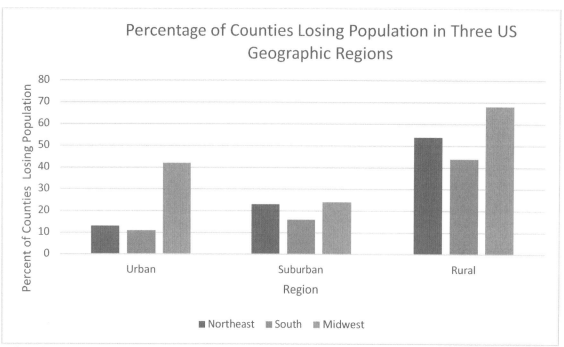

Percentage of Counties Losing Population in Three US Geographic Regions

Adapted from "Pew Research Center, May 2018, "What Unites and Divides Urban, Suburban and Rural Communities."

The Pew Research Center regularly conducts studies to examine population trends in the United States that result from changes in birth, death, and migration patterns. A 2018 report by Kim Parker and colleagues found that while there were regional variations in population shifts, rural counties in some regions of the country were especially prone to population loss; for example,_____

12. Which choice most effectively uses data from the graph to complete the example?
   (A) the proportion of rural counties with population decreases in the Northeast was roughly equal to the proportion of urban counties with population decreases in the Midwest.
   (B) the percentage of rural, urban, and suburban counties whose populations declined was least in the Northeast.
   (C) the majority of rural counties in the Northeast and Midwest saw their populations decrease, but a majority in the South did not.
   (D) a greater fraction of rural counties in the South than in the Northeast experienced net population loss.

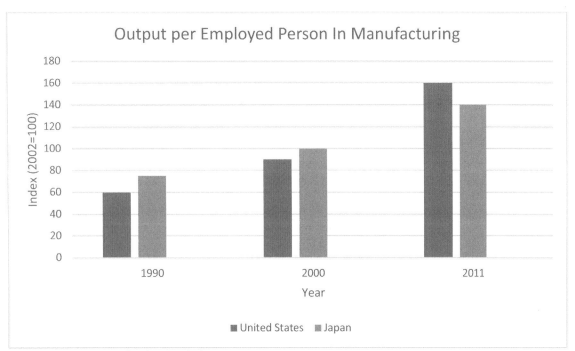

Output per Employed Person In Manufacturing

Source: U.S. Bureau of Labor Statistics

As technology becomes more advanced, there is some concern that human workers will become displaced. Although technology will certainly transform the nature of work in fields ranging from manufacturing to education to finance, Harvard economist Howard Katz asserts there will never be a shortage of jobs for people. Despite increases in automation, human factory workers in the United States and Japan have actually become more productive; for example, for the three years shown in the graph,_____

13. Which choice uses data from the chart to support the claim in the last sentence?

   (A) average output per worker in both countries was highest in 2000.

   (B) in terms of output produced, factory workers in Japan were more productive than those in the United States in 1990 but less productive in 2011.

   (C) the average output per worker didn't fluctuate from 1990 to 2000 for either country.

   (D) the output produced per worker increased in both countries from 1990 to 2011.

Year	Percentage of houses with internet access in 2006	Percentage of houses with internet access in 2010	Percentage of houses with internet access in 2015	Percentage of houses with internet access in 2021
Spain	38%	58%	79%	96%
France	41%	74%	83%	93%

Source: OECD

Spain and France have both seen a dramatic increase in the proportion of households with internet access during the 21st century. However, this transition happened at very different rates in each country. This can be seen most clearly by comparing the percentage of households in both countries with internet access in _____

14. Which choice most effectively uses data from the table to complete the sentence?

    (A) 2006 and 2021.

    (B) 2015 and 2021.

    (C) 2006 and 2010.

    (D) 2006 and 2015.

When a prominent museum hired a new curator in a large multicultural metropolis, one of the curator's aims was to strengthen the representation of Latin American artists, who had traditionally been underrepresented in the museum's exhibits. Some art history scholars claim the curator has been successful in her aims.

15. Which of the following, if true, would best support the claim of the art history scholars?

    (A) Since the new curator took over, the proportion of artwork at the museum's exhibitions that is by Latin American artists has increased by a substantial margin.

    (B) Some of the Latin American artists featured in the museum's exhibits had extensive conversations with the curator, explaining the inspiration behind their works.

    (C) The curator, who holds a Ph.D. in art history, has been interviewed by more major news publications since being appointed to her new position than she did before acquiring this position.

    (D) The curator, who herself is Latin American, has led efforts to attract more Latin American museumgoers to exhibits featuring artists of all different cultural backgrounds.

A study by Herman Pontzer found evidence that some dinosaur species may have been endothermic (warm-blooded) rather than ectothermic (cold-blooded). Pontzer made this conclusion in part based on an analysis of leg bones of 13 extinct dinosaur species, which allowed his team to estimate the metabolic requirements for walking and running. Based on an analysis of the likely locomotive costs of movement in relation to those for modern-day warm-blooded and cold-blooded animals, Pontzer concluded that the dinosaurs in his sample were likely warm-blooded. Pontzer argues that his findings support the idea that endothermy would allow dinosaurs to live athletic existences and range over wider areas than ectotherms would be able to during the Mesozoic Era.

16. Which choice, if true, best supports Pontzer's argument?

   (A) It is easier to estimate the likely metabolic costs land-dwelling dinosaur species incurred in walking based on analyses of their leg bones than it is to make comparable analyses for sea-dwelling ectotherms.
   (B) Remains of dinosaurs from the Mesozoic Era have been found over a significantly larger geographical range than those of known ectotherms.
   (C) Temperatures were considerably more hospitable for ectotherms in the coldest latitudes of Earth during the Mesozoic Era than they are for modern ectotherms.
   (D) Fossils of some known ectotherms from the Mesozoic Era have similar bone structures to certain species of dinosaurs included in Pontzer's study.

A painter, sculptor, and ceramicist, Pablo Picasso was one of the most renowned and prolific artists of the twentieth century. In an essay, one student claims that some of Picasso's works have deep political significance—he employed his artistic techniques as a political weapon to convey his deeply held convictions.

17. Which of the following, if true, would best support the student's claim?

   (A) In some of Picasso's artwork, he included symbols that conveyed his opposition to the actions committed by dictators and fascist political regimes.
   (B) Picasso himself was a devoted member of the Communist Party and a strong proponent of world peace.
   (C) Picasso founded Cubism, an art movement in which objects are often represented in abstracted form and from multiple viewpoints in order to depict subjects in more robust contexts.
   (D) Picasso analyzed traditional Western and Central African sculptures and artifacts, later integrating some of their stylistic and spiritual elements into his art.

It has long been debated whether purple sea urchins, *Strongylocentrotus purpuratus,* form their own pits in rocky temperate reefs or settle into existing ones. A study led by Michael P. Russell found that they do form pits of their own, breaking down rock surfaces such as granite and sandstone in a process known as bioerosion. A high school student hypothesized that sea urchins benefit not only from the shelter they receive from the pits they form but also from the process of creating pits themselves. That is, he believed the actual act of creating pits provides some sort of biological benefit for urchins, such as the production of chemicals that improve their health.

18. Which of the following, if true, would most directly support the high school student's hypothesis?

    (A) The same proportion of sandstone rocks in purple sea urchins' habitats covered by pits in the wild is comparable to the proportion of sandstone rocks in purple sea urchins' artificial laboratory habitats covered by pits.

    (B) Purple sea urchins serve a vital ecological niche by regulating kelp forest densities via algal grazing, enhancing the health of marine environments.

    (C) Purple sea urchins erode certain types of rocks, such as sandstone, much more quickly than they do other types of rocks, such as granite.

    (D) Even when placed in areas with more than sufficient pits to provide shelter, purple sea urchins will rapidly erode rocks.

It has long been known that many species of plants and mycorrhizal fungi are mutually dependent on each other for resources and survival. *Vicia faba* is a species of bean plant that produces toxins against harmful aphids (insects). A team of scientists hypothesized that an underground network of fungi protects the plants by sending chemical signals between attacked plants and other plants: this allows plants not being attacked to undergo biological changes that prepare them to ward off potential insect attackers. Indeed, plants not under attack themselves but that are connected to plants that are under attack do produce chemicals that repel aphids and attract helpful wasps, which consume the aphids.

19. Which of the following, if true, would best support the scientists' hypothesis?

    (A) Other species of bean plants have underground root systems similar in shape to those of *Vicia faba.*

    (B) Plants under attack but that are not connected to a fungal network are capable of producing chemicals that lure wasps.

    (C) *Vicia faba* plants not under attack and whose fungal connections to other plants are cut off will not produce chemicals that repel aphids.

    (D) Although many plants produce chemicals that repel aphids and attract wasps, the chemical composition of these chemicals varies.

In Willa Cather's 1918 novel *My Antonia*, she portrays the narrator Jim Burden has having a deep emotional connection with nature:_____.

20. Which quotation from *My Antonia* most effectively illustrates the claim?

(A) "When the straw settled down, I had a hard bed. Cautiously I slipped from under the buffalo hide, got up on my knees and peered over the side of the wagon. There seemed to be nothing to see; no fences, no creeks or trees, no hills or fields. If there was a road, I could not make it out in the faint starlight. There was nothing but land: not a country at all, but the material out of which countries are made."

(B) "I do not remember our arrival at my grandfather's farm sometime before daybreak, after a drive of nearly twenty miles with heavy work-horses. When I awoke, it was afternoon. I was lying in a little room, scarcely larger than the bed that held me, and the window-shade at my head was flapping softly in a warm wind."

(C) "The earth was warm under me, and warm as I crumbled it through my fingers. Queer little red bugs came out and moved in slow squadrons around me. Their backs were polished vermilion, with black spots. I kept as still as I could. Nothing happened. I did not expect anything to happen. I was something that lay under the sun and felt it, like the pumpkins, and I did not want to be anything more. I was entirely happy."

(D) "The road ran about like a wild thing, avoiding the deep draws, crossing them where they were wide and shallow. And all along it, wherever it looped or ran, the sunflowers grew; some of them were as big as little trees, with great rough leaves and many branches which bore dozens of blossoms. They made a gold ribbon across the prairie."

Many educators argue that providing quality feedback on student writing is a sophisticated skill that takes time to develop. With advances in artificial intelligence (AI), several studies have shown the potential of automated essay scoring to both grade and provide quality feedback to student writing that rivals the quality of a qualified human scorer. Some educational professionals worry that as educational technology becomes more sophisticated, they may become replaced by intelligent technology. Still, one expert says that such an outcome is highly unlikely.

21. Which research finding, if true, would best support the expert's claim?

(A) In one study, both automated essay scorers and human essay scorers failed to notice a similar number of spelling and grammatical errors.

(B) Technology that assumes certain educational functions traditionally done by educational professionals gives these professionals more time to focus on professional tasks that are best done by humans.

(C) A controlled experiment found that students learning from an artificial chatbot reported higher levels of motivation for learning than did a control group learning from a human lecturer.

(D) One study found that automated computer scorers were able to grade papers much more quickly than were their human counterparts.

Researchers Brynne C DiMenichi and Elizabeth Tricomi claim that competition—a performance situation in which success depends on performing better than others—can improve attention on tasks involving physical effort. In a study involving college students participating for course credit, participants had to perform an effort bar task in a computerized water gun game in two different conditions. In the "self" condition, participants had the opportunity to win bonus money if they won two thirds of trials against a clock. In the "competition" condition, participants were told they could win the bonus money if they beat a competitor in more games. Researchers measured reaction times of students in both the "self" and "competition" conditions, as faster reaction times are indicative of increased attention. Gender differences between males and females in both tasks were also compared.

22. Which finding from the researchers' study, if true, would most directly support their claim?
    (A) In a post-experiment survey, participants were more likely to report that the "competition" condition was more stressful than the "self" condition.
    (B) Males had faster reaction times than females, on average, regardless of the experimental condition.
    (C) Participants in the "self" condition were more likely to imagine how the bonus money would benefit their lives.
    (D) Participants had significantly slower press reaction rates in the "self" condition than in the "competition" condition.

According to psychologist Daniel Batson, empathic concern—feelings of sympathy or tenderness—compels people to act altruistically, or in ways that help others. In one study, subjects were asked to listen to a broadcast by a woman named Carol who claimed to be falling behind in class after an injury. Some students in a high-empathy experimental condition were told to focus on how Carol was feeling, prompting them to feel more empathetic. Other students in a low-empathy experimental condition were told to focus on the technical aspects of the broadcast and to ignore Carol's feelings, thus making it less likely that the students would feel high levels of empathy. Students in both groups were given the opportunity to agree to meet with Carol and provide her with help.

23. Which finding from Batson's study, if true, would most directly support his claim?
    (A) Students asked to focus on Carol's feelings during the broadcast were more likely to believe that Carol was genuinely struggling in the class than were students who were asked to focus on the technical aspects of Carol's broadcast.
    (B) Students who did not offer to help Carol were more likely to report feeling empathy towards Carol, regardless of whether they were prompted to focus on Carol's feelings or the technical aspects of her broadcast.
    (C) Students who were asked to focus on Carol's emotions during the broadcast were significantly more likely to offer to help Carol than were students who were asked to focus on the technical aspects of Carol's broadcast.
    (D) Students who were asked to disregard Carol's feelings during the broadcast were more likely to remember specific biographical details about Carol than were those who were asked to focus on her feelings.

As wolves began to migrate from Canada into the Northwestern United States, Charles Ripple and colleagues speculated that reintroducing wolves would have a cascading effect on local ecosystems. Specifically, they hypothesized that introducing wolves to an ecosystem with a large number of coyotes would cause the population of coyotes to decline, as wolves feed on coyotes. This in turn would release predation pressure on the coyote's prey, the lynx. Indeed, a study of Yellowstone Park showed that the number of coyotes in Yellowstone National Park decreased by over 50% in the first five years after wolves were introduced to the park.

24. Which of the following, if true, would most seriously undermine Ripple's hypothesis?

(A) In other major ecosystems outside of Yellowstone Park, there was a positive relationship between wolf reintroduction and coyote numbers, as coyotes fed off carcasses of wolf prey.

(B) Some sections of Yellowstone Park where wolves did not roam in large numbers had flourishing coyote populations and low lynx populations.

(C) Wolves in Yellowstone Park will often choose not to hunt coyotes they encounter if they have already fed on other prey, such as elk.

(D) At a site not included in the study, there are large wolf populations but no established lynx populations.

Scientists have hypothesized that a decline in sea otter and seal populations in southwest Alaska led to a decline in populations of kelp. Sea otters and seals do not generally feed on kelp, but they do feed on one of kelp's main predators, the sea urchin.

25. Which finding, if true, would most directly support the scientists' hypothesis?

(A) A decline in the population of seal and sea otters' prey other than urchins has been associated with a decline in sea otter populations.

(B) A decline in the population of seal and sea otters is associated with an increase in the population of sea urchins.

(C) Consumption of kelp by species other than sea urchins has increased before sea otters and seals saw their populations decline.

(D) Kelp populations tend to be highest in areas with thriving populations of sea urchins, regardless of sea otter and seal populations.

Country	2021 Urban Population Growth	2021 Economic Growth
Djibouti	1.6%	4.8%
Tunisia	1.3%	4.3%
Luxembourg	1.8%	5.1%
Somalia	4.4%	4.0%
Germany	0.2%	2.6%

Source: World Bank.

A pair of studies by Susanne A. Frick and Andrés Rodríguez-Pose of the London School of Economics examined the relationship between countries' rates of urbanization (growth of cities) and their rates of economic growth. They found that, while rapid urbanization once was associated with corresponding rapid economic growth, the relationship between the variables is not so simple. The researchers claim that two countries with very different urbanization rates can grow economically at about the same rate.

26. Which choice best describes data from the table that supports the researchers' claim for the year 2021?

(A) Luxembourg urbanized by a higher percentage than Djibouti, and its economy also grew by a higher percentage.

(B) Germany is the country in the table with both the lowest urban population growth and the lowest economic growth.

(C) Tunisia and Djibouti had a similar urban population growth percentage increase, but Tunisia's economy grew by a greater percentage.

(D) Somalia and Tunisia grew economically at similar rates despite Somalia urbanizing by a notably greater percentage.

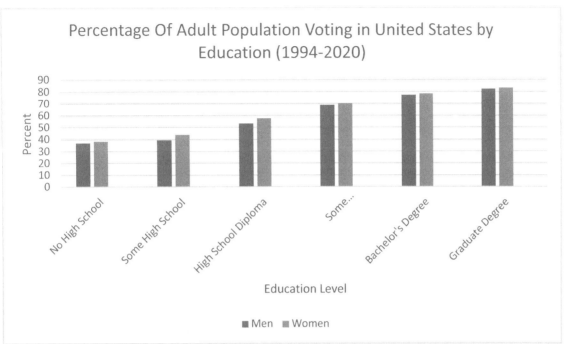

Percentage Of Adult Population Voting in United States by Education (1994-2020)

Source: Center for American Women and Politics.

Many scholars believe that differences in education are associated with a greater or lower likelihood of voting in national elections. Some researchers argued that education is positively associated with voting—that is, more educated voters are more confident in their ability to choose quality candidates.

27. Which of the following describes data from the graph to support the researchers' claims?

   (A) Among voters of the same gender, less educated voters vote at lower rates.

   (B) Only women voters with some high school education have voter turnout rates between 40% and 50%.

   (C) Among voters of the same educational level, women vote at higher rates than men.

   (D) Women are both more likely to have no high school education or an advanced degree than are men.

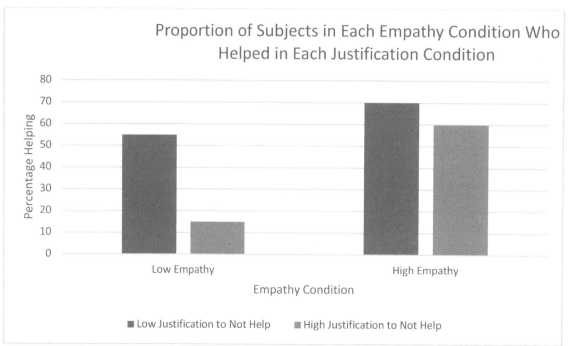

Proportion of Subjects in Each Empathy Condition Who Helped in Each Justification Condition

■ Low Justification to Not Help　■ High Justification to Not Help

Batson, C.D., Dyck, J.L., Brandt, J.R., Batson, J.G., Powell, A.L., Mcmaster, M.R., & Griffitt, C.A. (1988). Five studies testing two new egoistic alternatives to the empathy-altruism hypothesis. *Journal of personality and social psychology, 55 1*, 52-77.

Empathy altruists argue that prosocial behavior—actions done to help other people in need—is done out of genuine compassion, not out of a desire to obtain a personal benefit, such as to avoid social criticism or to reap social rewards. In one classic study, subjects were manipulated to feel high or low empathy for a distressed individual. Some subjects in each category were given a high justification (low personal cost to the helper) for not helping while others were given a low justification (high personal cost) for not helping. Based on the results, the researchers concluded that empathy is a powerful motivator.

28. Which choice best describes data from the graph to support the researchers' conclusions?
    (A) In both empathy conditions, subjects helped less when they had a higher justification for not helping.
    (B) Subjects in the high-empathy condition with a high justification for not helping helped more than individuals in the low-empathy condition with a low justification for not helping.
    (C) Low-empathy individuals helped more than half the time when there was a high personal cost to not helping.
    (D) High-empathy individuals helped less than 80% of the time even when there was a low justification for not helping.

Traditional arguments in political science attribute voter behavior to fixed preferences. For example, proponents of this view would argue that voters who care a lot about issues related to environmental protection are more likely to vote for candidates who support aggressive environmental legislation. According to the traditional view, the physical building where a person votes should not impact how he or she votes. But Jonah Berger was skeptical of the conventional wisdom, arguing that imagery in the locations where people vote send messages that could alter voting behavior (e.g., those voting in firehouses might be more likely to support measures increasing fire department funding). To test this idea, Berger and his colleagues examined voter data for people assigned to vote in various venues and analyzed how their voting patterns differed in Arizona's 2000 general election. They especially focused on a proposal to raise the sales tax from 5% to 5.6% in order to increase school funding.

29. Which finding from Berger's study, if true, would most directly undermine the traditional arguments about voting behavior?
    (A) Voters who did not vote in a school were significantly more likely to vote in favor of the measure to increase public school funding if they lived within 0.5 miles of a school than if they lived farther away from a school.
    (B) Controlling for demographic factors, subjects who lived within 0.2 miles of a school were more likely to support the increased sales tax for public school funding if they voted in a school than if they voted in a different type of venue.
    (C) Regardless of the venue in which one voted, a vote in favor of the sales tax hike to increase public school funding was strongly predicted by whether or not the voter had school-aged children enrolled in public schools.
    (D) Voters who voted in a school and voters who voted in other venues were more likely to vote to approve the sales tax hike to increase public school funding than they were to vote against the tax hike.

Latino and Latin American artists are often under-represented in art exhibits throughout the United States. When they are prominently featured, many critics gripe that it is traditionally to demonstrate how Latin American and Latino artists were influenced by European "high art" as a means of "elevating" their works. One journalist claims that some modern art curators are reversing this trend, making efforts to present Latin American and Latino artists in a way that counters this Eurocentric narrative.

30. Which of the following, if true, would most strengthen the journalist's claim?
    (A) The exhibit "Latin American Artists of the 20th Century" shows how various Latin American artists, such as Diego Rivera, adopted elements of European Modernism to break free from more conservative traditions of their local academies.
    (B) The exhibit "Come As You Are: Art of the 1990s" highlights works by artists from diverse racial and cultural backgrounds born or practicing in the United States, such as Gabriel Orozco and Shirin Neshat.
    (C) The exhibit "Popular Painters and Other Visionaries" features works by self-taught Latin American artists operating outside European Modernist traditions, including banners by Haitian priests reflecting local art conditions and Afro-Atlantic influences.
    (D) The exhibit "Radical Women: Latin American Art, 1960-1985" features works in a variety of mediums, such as traditional paintings and video art, and many of the featured artists have acted as political activists.

Composing, or writing music, is typically a solitary profession. Composers' collectives, such as the Sleeping Giant and The Bang on a Can, however, are groups of composers who come together to write music that is to be performed. Such collectives may be formed for a variety of practical and aesthetic reasons, such as to gain access to others' expertise or to feel less isolated in the writing process. A journalist claims, though, that these collectives often are rife with interpersonal conflicts between members.

31. Which quotation from an interview with a composers' collective member would best support the journalist's claim?
    (A) "It's tumultuous. Not only do we argue with each other, but we also consider different opinions far more than we should."
    (B) "It does mean that it takes longer. Because we'll email each other back and forth a hundred times a day. But it really is wonderful to not be in a vacuum when you are composing."
    (C) "We're not trying to promote any one aesthetic."
    (D) "People like commissioning us. It's a good way of ensuring that you'll have a cohesive piece."

It has conventionally been believed that geographic separation provides the catalyst for speciation, the process by which a single species evolves into separate, distinct species. Biologist Kate Langin noticed that the island scrub jay on Santa Cruz seems to have split into different habitats whose scrub jays rarely interbreed despite being located within a narrow geographic range, with shorter-billed scrub jays living in oak forests and longer-billed scrub jays living in pine forests. Langin hypothesizes that perhaps female scrub jays are attracted to male scrub jays with the same types of beaks as they have, a preference that over time will drive phenotypic and genetic differences between the subspecies, eventually resulting in them being separate species.

32. Which of the following, if true, would most directly support Langin's hypothesis?
    (A) Scrub jays communicate different messages with each other depending on their vocalizations, which themselves are modulated in part by beak length.
    (B) The foraging habits of pine forest and oak forest scrub jays have remained relatively consistent over the past century.
    (C) The shorter bills of the oak forest scrub bays are more suitable for opening up acorns.
    (D) Over several generations, the beaks of the oak forest male scrub jays have gotten shorter relative to those of the pine forest male scrub jays.

In Katherine Mansfield's short story, "An Ideal Family," the main character, Mr. Neave, is an old man who realizes he has spent so much of his life achieving business success that he barely understands his family, who largely take him for granted. In the story, Mansfield contrasts the alluring appearance of Mr. Neave's son Harold with his more unpleasant behavior.

33. Which quotation from "An Ideal Family" most effectively illustrates the claim about Harold?

(A) "Harold hadn't come back from lunch until close to four. Where had he been? What had he been up to? He wasn't going to let his father know."

(B) "Ah, Harold was too handsome, too handsome by far; that had been the trouble all along. As for his mother, his sisters, and the servants, it was not too much to say they made a young god of him; they worshiped Harold, they forgave him everything."

(C) "But it wasn't only his family who spoiled Harold, he reflected, it was everybody. So perhaps it wasn't to be wondered that he expected the office to carry on the tradition."

(D) "Where was Harold? Ah, it was no good expecting anything from Harold. Down, down went the little old spider, and then, to his horror, old Mr. Neave saw him slip past the dining-room and make for the porch, the dark drive, the carriage gates, the office. Stop him, stop him, somebody!"

An astronomer claims that dark matter—an invisible theoretical substance that does not emit light yet exerts a measurable gravitational influence on planets—is essential to galaxy formation. This assertion is based in part by computer models that suggest that galaxies are formed when dark matter merges and clusters together. The dark matter may act as a scaffolding in which normal (visible) matter in the galaxy resides.

34. Which finding, if true, does most to undermine the astronomer's claim?

(A) Dark matter is about five times as abundant as normal matter in the universe.

(B) Most spiral galaxies spin at a rate faster than can be explained by the mass of normal matter alone.

(C) Scientists disagree about what dark matter is made of, though most believe it is made of weakly interacting massive particles or axioms.

(D) Evidence emerges that galaxies without any dark matter exist.

In an essay, a student criticizes some historians for their celebration of Joan of Arc, a young woman who inspired the French army to go on to victory in the Hundred Years' War. The student claims that too many historians have focused on her status as a feminist icon.

35. Which quotation from a historian would best illustrate the student's claim?

(A) "Though historians continue to examine shards of her [Joan's] life, her reality remains elusive."

(B) "No figure from late medieval European history has generated as much modern popular interest, scholarly ink, and as many cinematic portrayals as the illiterate 'Maid of Lorraine' Joan of Arc."

(C) "Volumes can be written examining the attitudes of various historical figures and their image of Joan in relation to their ideas and achievements, some more puzzling than others."

(D) "Her [Joan's] image acts as a magic mirror of personal and political idealism and, in particular, of changing ideas about women's heroism."

In William Shakespeare's *Macbeth*, Lady Macbeth has her husband kill the King of Scotland in order for Macbeth to become king. While she is power-hungry and ambitious at the beginning of the play, she eventually becomes overcome with guilt for her crimes, as is evident when

_____

36. Which choice most effectively uses a quotation from *Macbeth* to illustrate the claim that Lady Macbeth felt remorse?
    (A) she says to herself, "Art not without ambition, but without/The illness should attend it."
    (B) she says to herself, "And fill me from the crown to the toe top-full
        Of direst cruelty!/ make thick my blood;/Stop up the access and passage to remorse,"
    (C) she says to Macbeth, "Your hand, your tongue: look like the innocent flower,
        But be the serpent under't."
    (D) she says to Macbeth, "Here's the smell of blood still/All perfumes of Arabia will not sweeten this little hand."

Altitude (meters above sea level)	MNE for Frogs Without UVB Exposure	MNE for Frogs With UVB Exposure
450	1	7
800	.5	5
1250	.5	3
2050	0	.2

Data adapted from Blaustein AR, Belden LK. Amphibian defenses against ultraviolet-B radiation. Evol Dev. 2003 Jan-Feb;5(1):89-97. doi: 10.1046/j.1525-142x.2003.03014.x. PMID: 12492415.

UVB radiation can have harmful effects on amphibians, such as by altering their DNA. However, Andrew Blaustein and Lisa Belden note that amphibians possess defenses to protect them against UVB damage or repair DNA once it has been damaged. They compared MNE frequency (micronucleated erythrocyte concentration per 100 erythrocytes) as an indication of DNA damage for frogs from the species *Rana temporaria* at various altitudes. Based on their findings, they concluded that high-altitude frogs likely have adapted to higher levels of UVB radiation, as_____. One hypothesis to account for the team's findings is that higher-altitude frogs may possess higher concentrations of DNA photolyase, an enzyme that repairs DNA.

37. Which choice most effectively uses data from the table to support the researchers' conclusion?
    (A) at each altitude, frogs that were not exposed to UVB radiation underwent less DNA damage than frogs who were exposed to such radiation.
    (B) frogs at an altitude of 2,050 meters and who were not exposed to UVB showed negligible DNA damage.
    (C) among frogs exposed to UVB radiation, those at higher altitudes showed less evidence of having experienced DNA damage.
    (D) the higher MNE values for frogs at 450 meters above sea level than for frogs at 800 meters above sea level suggests that the population of frogs is higher at higher altitudes.

Measure (mean, in seconds)	Breed				
	Ancient	Herding	Hound	Retriever	Working
Latency of the first gazing	29.90	18.96	17.41	12.52	14.86
Total gazing	4.28	12.80	13.59	17.12	14.90
Contact with the apparatus	36.71	33.27	29.98	22.98	30.87

Konno A, Romero T, Inoue-Murayama M, Saito A, Hasegawa T (2016) Dog Breed Differences in Visual Communication with Humans. PLoS ONE 11(10): e0164760. doi:10.1371/journal.pone.0164760

Previous research has suggested that the social skills of dogs have been aided by domestication, as they are more responsive to human social cues than are wolves raised by humans. Akitsugu Konno and colleagues hypothesized that "Ancient" dog breeds, which are most closely genetically related to wolves, would show less spontaneous gazing behavior to humans in an unsolvable task than would other breed groups (Herding, Hunting, Retrieving, Working). Dogs in the study were given an "unsolvable" task. Konno's team measured three behavioral variables: latency (time elapsed since the task started and the dog first tilted its head to turn to the owner or experimenter), total duration of time dogs spent gazing at a human, and the total duration of time dogs made physical contact with the apparatus involved in the task.

38. Which choice best describes data from the table to support the research team's hypothesis?

   (A) The Ancient breed dogs spent, on average, more than a minute making contact with the apparatus, while other breeds spent under a minute, on average, making contact with it.

   (B) All dog breeds spent less than half a minute, on average, gazing at a person during the experiment.

   (C) The Ancient breed dogs took longer to first look at a person during the task and spent less total time looking at a person during the task than did other dogs.

   (D) The Ancient dog breeds spent more time making contact with the apparatus than they spent gazing at a person during the experiment, on average.

Prize Amount (in dollars)	Median Number of Risks Taken in Baseline Condition	Median Number of Risks Taken in Rival Condition
5	9	10
10	7	12
25	4	10
30	2	7
40	3	6
45	1	8
50	2	9

A student recruited a random sample of college students who are fans of their school's football team to play a novel game that included "risky" opportunities, which could either double or halve their score, and "safe" opportunities that had more limited earning potential but less potential for drastic losses. Half the students played against people wearing hats from rival schools (the rival condition), and half played against strangers with no such hats (the baseline condition). Games were played for prizes ranging from $5 to $50. The student concluded that people are more willing to take risks against rivals out of a sense of competitiveness, as_____

39. Which choice most effectively uses data from the table to support the student's conclusion?

(A) for each prize amount, students in the rivalry condition seemed less risk averse.

(B) students in both competitive conditions were more likely to take more risks when the stakes were relatively low.

(C) students in the rival condition took the most risks when the prize was $10, suggesting they were most confident in their abilities when playing for a relatively low prize amount.

(D) students in the baseline condition had a better sense of how to gauge their chances of winning, as indicated by their conservative game play in higher-stakes games.

Plant	Average mass, in grams, of plants grown in soil without wood ash (less alkaline soil)	Average mass, in grams, of plants grown in soil with wood ash (more alkaline soil)
Garlic	30.5	39.2
Leeks	210.4	230.5
Potatoes	175.6	182.4

Wood ash can improve the growth of some plants that thrive in soil with a less acidic environment. A student conducts an experiment that includes some plants that are known to thrive when wood ash is included in its soil (garlic and leeks) and some plants that are known to thrive in more acidic environments (potatoes). All three plant types were grown in two types of soil under otherwise identical growing conditions: one with a neutral pH and one with wood ash. The student measured the average mass of all three plants in each condition after 4 weeks, and was surprised to observe that _____

40. Which choice most effectively uses data from the graph to complete the example?
   (A) the average mass of garlic grown with wood ash was greater than the average mass of garlic grown without wood ash.
   (B) the average mass of potatoes grown with wood ash was higher than the average mass of garlic grown with wood ash.
   (C) the average mass of potatoes grown without wood ash was slightly lower than the average mass of potatoes grown with wood ash.
   (D) the average mass of garlic was highest in soil designed to create a more alkaline environment, while the mass was lowest for leeks in such soil.

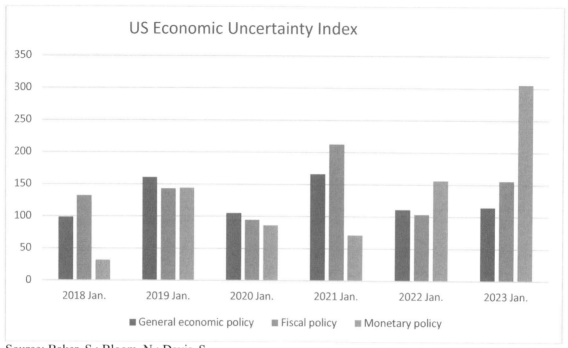

US Economic Uncertainty Index

Legend: ■ General economic policy ■ Fiscal policy ■ Monetary policy

Source: Baker, S.; Bloom, N.; Davis, S.

Economic uncertainty can be caused by many factors, such as political instability, changes in government policies, and market fluctuations. High levels of economic uncertainty can alter the behavior of economic actors in ways that are detrimental to the economy. For example, businesses may hire fewer workers or raise prices, and consumers might spend less money. When evaluating economic uncertainty, it is important to note that general measures of economic uncertainty might not reflect uncertainty in a specific economic policy area:_____

41. Which choice most effectively uses data from the graph to illustrate the claim?

   (A) general economic uncertainty was comparable to uncertainty in fiscal policy in January 2020 but differed from uncertainty about fiscal policy by a large value in January 2022.

   (B) general economic uncertainty was notably higher than uncertainty in monetary policy in January 2018 but substantially lower than uncertainty in monetary policy in January 2023.

   (C) general economic uncertainty reached its highest value in the same month that uncertainty about fiscal policy reached its lowest value.

   (D) general economic uncertainty was substantially lower than uncertainty about fiscal policy for each month represented on the graph.

Researcher Louis Deslauriers hypothesized that students would learn physics better when they engaged in active learning activities than when they listened to expert lectures, a form of passive learning. According to Deslauriers, listening to lectures on course content is less helpful to mastering the material than is actively working through practice problems with guided support from an instructor as needed. To test this hypothesis, Deslauriers conducted a study in which students in a college physics class were divided into two groups. Students in the control group were given a handout with blank spaces. They watched as an instructor lectured on the material and demonstrated how to solve problems, filling in their handouts as they listened. Students in the experimental group were given the same materials but had to attempt to solve the problems in small groups before being given the solutions.

42. Which of the following findings from the study, if true, would most strongly support Deslauriers's hypothesis?

(A) On average, students in the control group enjoyed the lectures more than students in the experimental group.

(B) On average, students in the control group were more likely to rate their instructor as effective.

(C) On average, students in the experimental group were more likely to report subjectively feeling as if they learned a lot in the lecture.

(D) On average, students in the control group scored lower on a test of learning following the lecture.

It has generally been believed that geographic isolation is a precondition for speciation, the process by which one species differentiates into two or more new species. Sympatric speciation is a more controversial idea, which argues that new species can evolve from a common species inhabiting the same geographic region. For instance, many scientists have noted that "resident" and "transient" ecotypes of orcas, though members of the same species and inhabitants of the same waters, consume different foods, have unique social structures, avoid contact with one another, and do not interbreed. Some scientists hypothesize that these orcas will one day be classified as distinct species that develop more pronounced genetic and phenotypic differences as they continue to avoid each other.

43. Which of the following, if true, would most directly support the hypothesis mentioned in the last sentence?

(A) Resident orcas have rounded tips on their dorsal fins, and transient orcas have more pointed dorsal fins.

(B) The breeding habits of resident and transient orcas have been relatively consistent over the past hundred years.

(C) Genetic diversity is high within both transient and resident orca populations.

(D) Over several generations, the diets of transient orcas have grown to be more diverse relative to those of resident orcas.

	Method Used	Correlation Absolute Value	Supports Weedman's Hypothesis?
A	Tool mass and spur count	-.100	Yes, but equivocal
B	Tool mass (as proxy for tool reduction) in relation to spur per uniface value	.943	Yes
C	Size-adjusted thickness (as proxy for tool reduction) in relation to spur count	.053	No
D	Size-adjusted thickness (as proxy for tool reduction) in relation to spur per uniface value	.257	No
E	Size-adjusted thickness (as proxy for tool reduction) in relation to spur presence or absence	.061	No

Adapted from *Eren MI, Jennings TA, Smallwood AM (2013) Paleoindian Unifacial Stone Tool 'Spurs': Intended Accessories or Incidental Accidents? PLoS ONE 8(11): e78419. doi:10.1371/journal.pone.0078419*

Sharp projections known as "spurs" on Paleoindian unifacial tools are thought by some scholars like Kathryn Weedman to be the results of accidents rather than the products of intentional design. Metin I. Eren and colleagues analyzed 563 tools and 629 tool fragments. They predicted that if this view is correct, the incidence of spurs correlates with tool reduction (as tools get smaller, spur presence should increase). Eren's team found that, depending on the proxy for tool reduction used to test their predictions, their results either supported the view that spurs were accidental or contradicted this view.

44. Which choice uses data from the table to best support Eren's team's conclusion?

(A) Measuring the correlation between size-adjusted thickness and spurs per uniface value yields much different results than using tool mass as a proxy for tool reduction to make this same correlation.

(B) Using tool mass as a proxy for tool reduction in relation to spurs per uniface value results in the highest correlation coefficient of the 5 trials.

(C) Using tool mass as a proxy for tool reduction better supports Weedman's hypothesis when analyzed in relation to spurs per uniface than when it is analyzed in relation to spur count.

(D) Size-adjusted thickness in relation to spur per uniface value produced a higher correlation coefficient than size-adjusted thickness in relation to spur presence or absence.

Type of Work	Known Number of Publications by Shakespeare
Plays	39: 16 (comedies), 11 (histories), 12 (tragedies)
Sonnets	154
Narrative Poems	3
Minor poems	3

A history student interested in the Elizabethan Era in England compiled a list of various literary works by William Shakespeare, including plays, sonnets, narrative poems, and smaller minor poems. However, because so many works from this era have likely not been accounted for—and many works that have been found have questionable authorship— the student argued that her table should be considered the smallest possible number of works authored by Shakespeare; in fact, _____

45. Which choice, if true, most effectively uses data from the table to complete the example?

    (A) three of the 16 comedies are regarded as "problem plays," lowering the number of true comedies to 13.

    (B) two unauthorized copies of Shakespeare's 154 known sonnets were published prematurely.

    (C) the actual number of plays Shakespeare wrote or contributed to is likely to be higher than 39, and he was believed to have collaborated with other writers.

    (D) some of Shakespeare's poems appeared in a collection called *The Passionate Pilgrim,* but only five of the 20 are accepted as being the works of Shakespeare.

Group	Treatment	Approximate Growth (in centimeters)
1	Water	60
2	Water+Salt	38
3	Water+Salt+Bacteria Species	52
4	Water+Salt+Marine Algae Species	47

Figure 1: The data in the table is adapted from Nabti, E., Sahnoune, M., Ghoul, M. et al. Restoration of Growth of Durum Wheat (Triticum durum var. waha) Under Saline Conditions Due to Inoculation with the Rhizosphere Bacterium Azospirillum brasilense NH and Extracts of the Marine Alga Ulva lactuca . J Plant Growth Regul 29, 6–22 (2010). https://doi.org/10.1007/s00344-009-9107-6.

A group of researchers estimated that seedlings for a wheat plant would grow approximately 65 centimeters 75 days after irrigation with water under a certain set of soil conditions without salt. Seedlings from wheat plants were randomly divided into groups, each under different sets of growing conditions. Some groups were treated with salt. Two of those groups were treated with an additional species (a species of bacteria or marine algae). Based on their results, the researchers concluded that salt stunted plant growth but that the inclusion of certain species of bacteria or marine algae could have a beneficial effect on plant growth that counteracts salt's stunting effect.

46. Which choice best describes data from the table to support the researchers' claim?
   (A) Plants in all four groups did not exceed 65 centimeters in growth.
   (B) Plants grown in Group 3 grew taller than those grown in Group 4.
   (C) Plant growth was lower for plants grown with salt than for plants grown without salt, and growth was higher for plants in Group 3 and 4 than for those in Group 2.
   (D) For plants in Group 2, plant growth was lower than would be expected in conditions without salt, and for plants in Groups 3 and 4, plant growth was higher than would be expected in soil conditions without salt.

In "Ode to the West Wind" by Percy Bysshe Shelley, the poet asks the wind to spread his ideas to other people, writing,_____

47. Which quotation from "Ode to the West Wind" best illustrates this claim?
   (A) "Thou, from whose unseen presence the leaves dead/
      Are driven, like ghosts from an enchanter fleeing,"
   (B) "Wild Spirit, which art moving everywhere;/
      Destroyer and Preserver; hear, O hear!"
   (C) "As thus with thee in prayer in my sore need./
      Oh! lift me as a wave, a leaf, a cloud!"
   (D) "Scatter, as from an unextinguished hearth/
      Ashes and sparks, my words among mankind!"

It was long believed that the Minoans, a Bronze Age civilization on modern-day Crete, descended from Egyptian refugees 5,000 years ago, but many archaeologists were skeptical of this idea. In a study led by geneticist George Stamatoyannopoulos, ancient mitochondrial DNA recovered from Cretan caves found that instead, the DNA of Minoans overlapped most with that of modern Europeans. The implication was that Minoan Crete was largely populated by people indigenous to the island. Stamatoyannopoulos claims that his team's findings are limited because_____

48. Which of the following, if true, best supports Stamatoyannopoulos's claim?

   (A) some tombs discovered on Crete have more resemblance to those of ancient Egypt than those of ancient Greece.

   (B) DNA from a few samples was too contaminated to be interpretable.

   (C) mitochondrial DNA only reveals information about maternal genetic lineages.

   (D) it is possible that cultural exchanges led to the discovery of Egyptian artifacts on Crete.

A student argues that one theme of Jean Toomer's poem "Storm Ending" is that tumultuous experiences eventually come to an end and can even lead to healing. Toomer illustrates this point with a metaphor to a powerful storm that eventually subsides: _____

49. Which of the following quotes from the poem best illustrates this claim?

   (A) "Thunder blossoms gorgeously above our heads."

   (B) "Rumbling in the wind/Stretching clappers to strike our ears."

   (C) "Bleeding rain."

   (D) "Dripping rain like golden honey."

Pre-Lesson Reflection Activity

Read the paragraph below about a concept known as "desirable difficulties."

Much research has been done into the science of how people learn effectively. One consistent finding has been that **"desirable difficulties,"** learning experiences that require substantial effort, promote better learning. For example, subjects learning new information in a laboratory setting typically have an easier time memorizing information when they take practice quizzes (which require active engagement) than when they read over the information. Other types of desirable difficulties include elaboration (explaining material in your own words and drawing connections), spaced practice (practicing the same material after a delay), and interleaved practice (varying order in which material is practiced), to name a few.

For the subject or topic of your choice, imagine how a teacher could design a lesson that incorporates desirable difficulties.

There are various inferences you can make about practices that exemplify desirable difficulties. Below are some potential suggestions.

1) In a vocabulary unit, have students pair up to engage in a verbal or text message conversation using words from the unit.
2) For a psychology class, have students create their own practice exams and quiz each other.
3) In a history class, have students complete a low-stakes practice quiz at the beginning of each class to prepare for a unit exam.
4) In a math class, have students alternate between drilling 2-3 topics for one homework assignment.
5) In a physics class, have students complete challenging word problems in groups.
6) In a biology class, have students explain in their own words how a biological process works.
7) In band, have students slowly practice scales and harder passages from advanced pieces to master technique.
8) In a hockey lesson, add more intense strength and conditioning drills that will help make performing the sport easier.

All of the above are just some of the logical implications a proponent of desirable difficulties might draw, as each involves creating effortful learning in an applied setting. Using some baseline information, we drew conclusions about possible implications of the research. When we draw conclusions that are not directly stated in a passage, we are making **inferences**.

We make inferences in our daily lives all the time without even realizing it. For example, if you see people at a table in a restaurant laughing loudly, you can probably infer that they are reacting to something perceived as funny. If you hear the sound of a guitar behind a door, you can infer someone is either playing guitar nearby or that at a recording of one is playing. If two celebrities who are well-known friends suddenly unfollow each other on all their social media accounts, you might infer they likely had some sort of falling out or that there might be some tension between them.

Inference questions on the SAT require you to draw logical conclusions about information that is **implied**, or hinted at, in the passage. These can be some of the most intimidating questions, as they require a bit of analysis, but with a methodical approach, most can be answered relatively easily.

To approach inference questions, do the following:
1) Read the passage carefully, keeping track of the baseline information that you are given. The passages are all very short, but underlining key details can still be helpful. **In brief, determine what the passage literally says.**
2) In your own words, consider what are the logical implications that might follow from that information. **In brief, think about what this information tells us must be true.** The leap of logic you make should not be so large as to require mountains of new evidence.
3) Systematically go through each choice, seeing if any match your predictions. Eliminate any choices that are contradicted by the given information, are not relevant to the given information, or that would require additional evidence.

The process of making an inference should stick as close to the text as possible.
Consider the following situation.
- **A German museum showcased a painting, claiming that it was the work of acclaimed artist Claude Monet.**
- **Some government officials suspected the painting might be a fake, as it included a preliminary sketch underneath the oil paintings, which was not typical of Monet's style.**
- **The painting was discovered to have oils meant to simulate the aging process.**
- **The painting had two signatures in different colors, which would be highly unusual for an authentic painting.**

Given the evidence that the painting was inconsistent with Monet's style and was treated with material designed to make it look older than it really was, the logical conclusion is that the painting was most likely a forgery and not a genuine Monet.

When making inferences, you want to avoid falling for common trap answers. Common traps include the following:
1) **Trap 1:** Choices that use language that is too extreme.
For example, if a passage implies that some people's health would improve if all restaurants listed the calorie contents of unhealthy foods, an extreme answer choice might say **most** people's health would improve if restaurants adopted this practice. Maybe some people will order unhealthy foods anyway or see their health remain the same or decline for other reasons (such as because they do not exercise).

2) **Trap 2:** Answer choices that are plausible (could reasonably be true) but go beyond the text.
For example, when a passage discusses the evidence that two ancient societies traded with one another, an answer choice that states either of them traded with additional societies would require more evidence. It is possible the societies had no other trading partners.

Mini Activity 2: Practice Drawing Conclusions

For each situation, practice predicting conclusions in your own words. Don't worry too much about identifying a single "right" answer. There may be more than one logical inference to be made from each situation.

Situation 1: Follow a Hypothesis

1) *Ephedra foeminea* is a Mediterranean shrub that reproduces by secreting droplets of pollen from its cones, a process requiring energy.
2) Catarina Rydin hypothesized *Ephedra foeminea*'s pollination cycle was connected to the lunar cycle, as insects that aid in spreading the pollen may use the moon to navigate.
3) Rydin noticed that *Ephedra foeminea*, which did not open its cones for several days, did open on the night of the full moon when the moon is brightest.
4) Though the light of a half moon is bright enough to guide insects, only during the full moon is the moon out all night.
5) Rydin would likely speculate that the *Ephedra foeminea* did not engage in its pollen display on the half-moon night because_____

Situation 2: Analyzing the Past

1) The Polynesians invented the double-hulled canoe, which allowed them to travel far distances.
2) Researchers have long wondered if prehistoric Polynesians and Native Americans made any contact.
3) A study by Alexander Ioannidis confirms that modern-day people living in Easter Island and four other Polynesian islands carry DNA from people who lived in South America 800 years ago.
4) The findings of the study suggest that _____

Situation 3: Solving a Puzzle

1) Scientists have long been confused why the frontal cortices of humans' brains are larger than one would predict for an average mammal of the same size.
2) Some scientists have noted that primates with the largest frontal cortices also have the most complex social networks and are the most intelligent.
3) A study showed hyenas with the simplest social systems also have the least developed frontal cortices.
4) When humans think about other people and social situations, their frontal cortices are more active.
5) This research supports the hypothesis that larger brains are needed for humans to

_____

Situation 4: Making a Value Judgment

1) Extraverts (people who are more outgoing and sociable) are often thought to make the best salespeople.
2) A study by Adam Grant at the University of Pennsylvania found extraverts generated less money in sales than did introverts (less talkative and sociable people).
3) Ambiverts (people neither overly extraverted or introverted) were the most successful salespeople.
4) Grant speculated that extraverts might rub customers the wrong way, such as by being too pushy and failing to listen.
5) One implication of this study might be is that employers of salespeople who are extraverts should _____

For the first situation, a logical inference is that the moon is not out long enough during the half moon, since the moon is bright enough to guide insects. Maybe the shrub is conserving its energy for a night when pollination is most likely to be successful.

For the second situation, a logical inference is that the ancient Polynesians and Native Americans made contact at some point, as evidenced by the mixing of their DNA. There could be multiple explanations for how the groups came into contact. Maybe the Polynesians met the Native Americans in South America, or perhaps South Americans traveled to Polynesia or went to Polynesia on Polynesian boats.

For the third situation, given that the size of the frontal cortex seems associated with the complexity of social networks, this might suggest the cortex plays a role in managing social relations or social intelligence.

For the fourth situation, an implication might be that bosses should hire more ambiverts or provide training to their salespeople with professional development in how to listen better and be less pushy.

Next, let's apply the inference skills used in this activity to test-like passages.

Sample 1

A study led by Kan Okano examined the relationship between sleep quality and academic performance. As part of this study, 100 students in a college chemistry class were given activity trackers that allowed multiple levels of sleep quality to be related to academic performance on exams and quizzes. The study found that student grades positively correlated with sleep duration in the month leading up to an exam when the unit was being taught, but not to sleep duration the night before the exam. With the caveat that the study cannot definitely draw conclusions about cause and effect, the researchers stated a tentative implication of this finding might be that

_____

Which of the following most logically completes the text?

   A) students in the class who had the highest scores generally made an intentional effort to sleep more in the weeks leading up to an exam in order to better retain information learned.
   B) quality of sleep during the time in which content is learned may be more important to academic performance than is quality of sleep in the time immediately before testing.
   C) most students in the class who did not earn perfect scores would probably have scored at least slightly higher with even one more hour of sleep the night before the exam.
   D) fluctuations in sleep cycles of different students affect different students differently.

We learn that students who got more sleep in the month leading up to an exam generally performed better than those who did not. The quality of sleep the night before the exam itself seemed to have no bearing on how students performed. An implication might be that quality sleep in the time when a unit is being taught helps students learn better so that they can perform better on exams.

Choice A might seem plausible at first glance, but it seems to take an extreme leap of logic that would require a bit more information. While students who got better sleep in the month leading up to an exam did generally score higher than peers who did not get as much sleep, there is nothing in the text to suggest that students slept more hours *with the intention* of enhancing their learning. Maybe these students would have gotten more sleep anyway.

Choice B seems like a good answer that nicely matches our prediction. Though we cannot definitely say there is a causal relationship, the association between improved sleep during the time in which material is learned and academic performance could suggest that sleep quality during the learning period is more important to academic performance than is sleep quality the night before an exam. **This is the correct choice**.

Choice C seems contradicted by the passage. The study found no relationship between sleep duration the night before an exam and performance, so it is unlikely the authors would draw this conclusion. Even if there had been a generally positive relationship, it would be a bit of stretch to say one more hour of sleep would increase performance.

Choice D is probably a true statement in the real world. However, it is not directly relevant to the passage's findings. The passage makes no discussion of how different people are differentially affected by sleep cycle fluctuations.

Sample 2

It has long been argued that human beings were primarily responsible for the extinction of wooly mammoths, a furry, long-tusked mammal related to modern elephants, through humans' excessive hunting of these creatures. This belief was partially based on the observation that mammoths had survived changes in climate for millions of years yet disappeared relatively quickly once humans came to the scene. Humans ate them as part of their diet, utilized their skeletons to construct shelters, and used their tusks to make harpoons. A team of biologists from the University of Cambridge sequenced environmental DNA from plant and animal remains and found that much of the vegetation on which the mammoth depended for survival had disappeared in the wake of climatic shifts after the last Ice Age, and the model showed humans had nothing to do with this. Therefore, the team concluded that_____

Which of the following most logically completes the text?
A) any animal species that has gone extinct in the past 4,000 years after being hunted by humans was already vulnerable primarily as a result of limited access to quality nutrition stemming from climate change.
B) the failure of mammoths to adapt to the Earth's changing ecology during the last Ice Age absolves humans of all responsibility in placing pressures on their population.
C) the extinction of mammoths cannot be fully attributable to the actions of human hunters.
D) if early humans had known that the mammoth's population was critically endangered, they would probably not have hunted them as intensely.

The main implication of the study is that humans likely did not hold primary responsibility for the mammoth's decline. Changing vegetation as a result of climatic factors seemed to play a significant role.

Choice A goes beyond the scope of the passage. We cannot draw conclusions about animals other than mammoths.

Choice B is too extreme. While humans were likely not fully responsible for mammoths' disappearance, the fact that they did hunt mammoths may suggest they at the very least accelerated their disappearance.

Choice C is correct. The new study implies that climate change was a more serious threat to mammoths.

Choice D is not supported by the passage, though it may be true. The passage gives no textual evidence to suggest humans hunted mammoths in large numbers because they believed they were not endangered. Maybe they would have kept hunting them anyway out of necessity.

Sample 3

Many aspiring writers or people who have strong opinions on certain issues will pen op-eds, short opinion pieces featured in publications ranging from newspapers to college websites. One expert argued that, unlike journal articles, which are more academic in nature, op-eds are more compelling when they include examples of personal anecdotes. Even if the piece includes references to research studies— such as the effectiveness of certain educational interventions if the writer is an education researcher or teacher—personal stories can humanize the author, grab the interest of readers, and allow readers to live vicariously through them. Personal stories can therefore_____.

Which of the following logically completes the text?
    A) allow op-ed writers to argue opinions without having to consult factual sources.
    B) help writers improve the quality of their opinion pieces.
    C) ensure that the arguments opinion writers put forth are grounded in reality.
    D) make laypeople understand the prose of op-eds that would otherwise be inaccessible.
The main argument is that personal stories can make op-eds stronger, such as by grabbing the reader's attention.

Choice A is not supported by the passage. An op-ed writer can consult factual sources with or without including personal stories.

Choice B is correct. The text argues for the benefits of including personal stories in op-eds. Thus, they can improve the quality of the pieces produced.

Choice C is a distortion. While personal stories can add true information grounded in personal experience, it is still possible to produce a factual article without references to a personal story.

Choice D is also a distortion. While personal stories can make the pieces more engaging to laypeople, they are not necessary for people to understand the texts.

A small magazine company was able to cut most of its costs after switching primarily to a digital service model. The cost savings were primarily in printing and distributing, which happen after the artwork, writing, and editing is complete. This suggests that_____.

1. Which of the following most logically completes the text?

   (A) the costs of artwork, writing, and editing were less impacted by the switch to a digital service model than were the costs of printing and distributing.

   (B) most consumers expect a discount for digital subscriptions of the magazine.

   (C) digital technologies have made it easier for writers to create longer and more creative stories.

   (D) the magazine decreased its budget for staff writers and editors.

In 1988, Robert Bakker and colleagues discovered a small tyrannosaur skull that they believed belonged to a unique species, called *Nanotyrannus,* a distinct species from the larger *Tyrannosaurus rex*. The decision to rule this skull as a member of a unique species was primarily based on an analysis of the fusion of its skull bones, which can roughly estimate the age of a dinosaur. Since all the bones appeared to be fused, researchers concluded the animal was a small adult. However, some researchers noted that the timing between sutures between skull bones varies by species, and the discovered skull exhibited some features characteristic of juveniles, such as large, round eye sockets. These researchers suggest that the skull might actually be that of a juvenile *Tyrannosaurus rex* rather than that of a separate adult species, as the method Bakker's team used for estimating the age of the skull _____

2. Which of the following most logically completes the text?

   (A) is merely the most reliable of a set of unreliable methods.

   (B) is rarely of any value to scientists studying the age of dinosaur skulls.

   (C) might not accurately reflect the true biological age of the skull.

   (D) is generally more effective for analyzing the age of dinosaur skulls than that of other animals.

When judges make rulings on cases before them, they are expected to impartially apply legal principles without being clouded by personal biases related to their own cultural backgrounds. However, Justice Sonia Sotomayor once argued that while judges should faithfully and fairly rule in all cases involving people of different backgrounds, attempts by men of color and women to ignore their personal experiences might ultimately do the law and society a disservice, as their unique personal experiences may better situate them to notice certain relevant facts in certain cases. She suggests that demographic differences between judges thus _____.

3. Which of the following most logically completes the text?

   (A) ensure that legal principles are applied equitably in most cases.

   (B) are essential to ensuring that the judicial system operates ethically.

   (C) have potential to benefit the general public without compromising the law.

   (D) lead to a regrettable situation that prevents judges from ruling without drawing on personal sympathies and prejudices.

Planetary scientists discovered what they believed to be evidence of "cryovolcanoes" on Saturn's largest moon Titan, which could explain the presence of methane in its atmosphere. These volcanoes form when water filters through the sides of a mount until it solidifies. This conclusion was made after NASA's Cassini spacecraft found what seemed to be surface features indicative of volcanic activity, including a pit resembling a large crater that seems to have been caused by a volcanic explosion. However, other scientists note that wind, water, and meteorite impacts would have similar impacts on the lunar surface. Therefore, _____

4. Which of the following most logically completes the text?

   (A) modern surface features on Titan do not necessarily reflect volcanic activity.
   (B) it is almost certain that something other than volcanic activity is responsible for the large crater the Cassini spacecraft observed on Titan.
   (C) multiple geologic forces interacted to produce the apparent signatures of volcanic activity on Titan.
   (D) methane was emitted from multiple volcanoes on Titan's surface.

Many herbaceous plant species require enough light so that photosynthesis can occur but not so much heat that they dry out and become overheated. Excessive heat is often associated with less efficient photorespiration, an energy-intensive process that removes toxins from plants. As part of a study led by Marina Semchenko, 46 temperate grassland species were exposed to the same growing conditions, but some plants were grown with shade cloths that blocked some sunlight while others were left uncovered. The researchers found that plants grown with a shade cloth that exposed them to 50% shade grew significantly more in mass than did plants not grown in shade, which might suggest that these species _____

5. Which choice most logically completes the text?

   (A) undergo most efficient photorespiration when they are exposed to frigid temperatures.
   (B) are some of the few types of plant species that can withstand high levels of irradiance.
   (C) can grow effectively under the presence of a shade cloth as long as the cloth is not too thin.
   (D) experience less thermal stress as a result of lower light intensity in the presence of a shade cloth.

It has long been known that migratory birds make stopovers in order to refuel. However, a study by biologist Arne Hegemann is the first to show birds also stop to strengthen their immune systems. It had previously been thought that when migrating birds stop in place for a few days to rest and eat, that it was to build up fat reserves. Migration itself is a physically taxing activity, subjecting birds to many pathogens while tiring them out. The study showed that various species of migratory birds such as chaffinches and dunnocks saw their immune systems build up the ability to attack bacteria and pathogens during these rest stops. These gains had no relationship to birds' fat levels. Instead, the researchers speculated that_____

6. Which choice most logically completes the text?
   (A) small migratory birds derive no marginal benefit from additional fat stores.
   (B) the immune boosts were associated with a break from migratory strains.
   (C) the only reason migratory birds take short breaks is to strengthen their immune systems.
   (D) lower fat levels might actually serve birds better in fighting off infections.

Oxford researchers were interested in learning how the brain responds to works of art when people are given information about their authenticity. When subjects believed they were looking at genuine Rembrandt paintings—regardless if they were actually real—subjects showed increased activity in regions of the brain associated with receiving rewards, such as sugary food or money. When subjects were told paintings were forgeries—even if they were actually genuine—subjects showed heightened activity in regions of the brain associated with strategic thinking as well as those associated with visual processing. Subjects did report trying to work out why the paintings they were looking at were fakes, supporting this finding. Interestingly, there were no meaningful differences between how subjects' brains responded to authentic works they believed were authentic and copies they believed were authentic. The researchers concluded that

7. Which choice most logically completes the text?
   (A) aesthetic judgments about works of art are determined by a single brain region's response to art rather than by a complex interaction between different brain regions.
   (B) the beauty of a work of art is primarily responsible for how rewarding viewers find it.
   (C) when many people are told that a work of art they find aesthetically pleasing is a forgery, their brains process the painting as visually unappealing.
   (D) aesthetic judgments about works of art are modulated in part by factors other than the visual content of the artwork.

A 2011 census by David Bennett shocked astronomers when it estimated the number of free-floating Jupiter mass gas giant planets to be twice as large as that of stars for a section in the Milky Way Galaxy. The survey was not sensitive to smaller Earth-sized planets. Based on the known methods for how planets of Jupiter's size become free-floating, this estimate seemed too large to many scientists. A subsequent study by Przemek Mróz estimated that there are only about 0.25 floating Jupiter-sized planets for every typical star. Interestingly, the study also found evidence for more brown dwarf stars than Bennett's study did. Brown dwarf stars bear a striking resemblance to Jupiter. Therefore, it seems plausible that _____

8. Which choice most logically completes the text?

(A) Bennett's census likely yielded a much higher number of floating Jupiter-sized planets than did Mróz's because Bennett failed to account for mechanisms that account for how gas giants become free-floating.

(B) there is some overlap in specific celestial bodies that Bennett's team classified as floating Jupiter-sized planets and that Mróz's classified as brown dwarfs.

(C) some differences between Earth-like planets and Jupiter-like planets may have been treated like variations within Jupiter-like planets by Bennett's team.

(D) the lack of precise measuring instruments for differentiating between brown dwarf stars and gas giant planets likely led Bennett to overestimate the number of brown dwarf stars.

There has long been debate over what caused fractures on Phobos, one of Mars's moons. For instance, some scientists believe the fractures are remnants from a single impact while others argue that they were caused by smaller strings of secondary impacts. One hypothesis, that the grooves were caused by tidal structures, had been disregarded by many scientists for a long time. This was largely based on the belief that tidal forces would not be strong enough to fracture a solid moon of Phobos's size. The tidal hypothesis has more recently gained traction with the discovery that the interior of Phobos might be much weaker than scientists had initially thought, suggesting that_____

9. Which choice most logically completes the sentence?

(A) single-impact events and chains of secondary impacts leave noticeably different indentations on rocky moon surfaces.

(B) tidal forces might have been powerful enough to cause the types of grooves present on Phobos.

(C) fluctuations in tidal forces affect moons of different compositions differently.

(D) tidal forces probably would not be able to crack the surface of Phobos at all had Phobos's composition been even the slightest bit denser.

While Shakespeare is perhaps best known for his tragic plays, such as *Hamlet, Macbeth,* and *Romeo and Juliet,* he also contributed a number of notable comedies to the literary canon. Unlike most Shakespearean tragedies, which typically feature characters who are members of the nobility confronting issues related to revenge, supernatural elements, and the struggle between good and evil, his comedy plays like *A Midsummer Night's Dream*—his most widely performed play today— typically portray common people. Though Shakespeare's comedies include lighthearted elements—like clever wordplay and witty insults—they also explore timeless, universal themes such as love, marriage, family, and friendship. Consequently, _____

10. Which statement most logically completes the text?
    (A) many audience members might find characters in many of Shakespeare's comedies generally more relatable than those in many of his tragedy plays.
    (B) most Shakespearean comedies are likely more accessible to audiences than modern-day comedies.
    (C) experts in theater history tend to prefer Shakespeare's comedies to all his other works.
    (D) *A Midsummer Night's Dream* is the Shakespearean comedy with the most timeless themes.

Gross Domestic Product (GDP), a standard measure of a country's economic growth, is sometimes considered a proxy for a nation's economic well-being and overall standard of living. It looks at measures such as consumption, private investment, government spending, and exports of products. Notably, GDP does not account for the distribution of economic activity within a country and thus cannot account for income inequality. For example, if the top 20% of income earners in a country see their wages skyrocket but the bottom 60% see little to no increase in their wages, overall GDP may still go up. GDP also does not examine many issues relevant to people's overall quality of life, such as environmental degradation and health outcomes. For example, Dr. Amit Kapoor notes that the number of cars counts positively towards GDP, while harmful emissions do not count negatively towards this measure. Thus, _____

11. Which statement most logically completes the sentence?
    (A) GDP is not a reliable measure of the extent to which most of a country's residents thrive.
    (B) income inequality and environmental justice issues are the two primary metrics that capture the quality of a nation's standard of living.
    (C) a country's economic output itself does not reveal any information about a nation's economic strength.
    (D) nations that have a relatively equitable distribution of wealth must have low GDP measures.

In the United States Congress (the legislative body of the United States), lawyers have long been overrepresented. In fact, conditional on running, lawyers who run for elections win at around double the rate as candidates from non-legal backgrounds do. Prevailing theories argue that voters are more likely to reward candidates with legal experience, which is relevant to the job of lawmakers. However, Adam Bonica disagrees with this conventional wisdom. One possible explanation for lawyers' overrepresentation in Congress is that lawyers running for election tend to have larger professional networks than non-lawyers that help them with campaign fundraising, and access to such funding _____

12. Which statement most logically completes the sentence?
   (A) alters the typical relationship between legal experience and subsequent career decisions by retiring lawyers.
   (B) encourages non-lawyers considering running for office to consider applying to law school instead.
   (C) makes it especially likely that candidates with professional experience as lawyers will have a competitive advantage over other candidates in waging effective campaigns that persuade voters.
   (D) has been used to motivate Congress to limit membership in many of its committees to those with professional legal experience.

Scholars have long noted Robert Merton's work on the Matthew Effect— a sociological phenomenon that explains the tendency of people to accrue success in proportion to their initial advantages— was based on part due to data supplied by his wife, fellow sociologist Harriet Zuckerman. However, such scientists failed to recognize that she is an accomplished scholar in her own right, and Merton later admitted that she deserved co-authorship credit for their research on the Matthew Effect. Thus, those who continue to regard Zuckerman as a mere assistant to her husband _____

13. Which statement most logically completes the sentence?
   (A) overlook the many factors inspiring Merton's research.
   (B) downplay the extent of Zucker's scholarly contributions to findings on the Matthew Effect.
   (C) misunderstand the tendency of sociologists to work in pairs on major projects.
   (D) are prone to misinterpreting the nuances of Merton and Zuckerman's joint research findings.

The Mycenaean civilization (c. 1600-1100 BCE), which occupies what is now mainland Greece, made use of Egyptian expertise and materials to produce a variety of their own goods. However, it seems that Mycenaeans did not acquire much of their knowledge directly from the Egyptians. Excluding the possibility that Mycenaeans independently started employing the same production methods as ancient Egyptians, these findings might suggest that_____

14. Which finding most logically completes the text?

(A) another group who did have more direct contact with the Egyptians passed on Egyptian products and knowledge to the Mycenaeans.

(B) Egyptians had no interest in learning about Mycenaean cultural practices.

(C) the products typically made by Egyptians required less sophisticated technologies than those made independently by Myceneans.

(D) Greek civilization only began to appreciate the extent to which Egyptians shaped it after the decline of the Mycenaean civilization.

Among social animals that live in broods, woodpecker finches appear to have an innate aptitude for tool use. Sabine Tebbich and colleagues divided broods of chicks into two groups, half of which were raised with a tool-using model by adult finches and half of which were not. Both groups developed similar abilities to use tools and reached similar developmental milestones, suggesting that _____

15. Which statement most logically completes the sentence?

(A) watching adult finches use tools does not yield any educational benefits to any individual chick.

(B) the ability to acquire tool usage skills seems to have an innate component in woodpecker finches that is not entirely dependent on social learning.

(C) most other animals that live in broods, such as primates, do not require adult instruction in order to master tool-using behavior.

(D) woodpecker finch chicks are just as skilled as adult woodpecker finches in making and using tools.

A psychology student wanted to know if aerobic exercise would improve performance on tasks related to cognitive abilities. However, he did not control for differences in the task difficulty. The cognitive abilities of subjects who performed easy puzzles requiring little effortful thinking were judged by the same standards as those who performed more challenging tasks that imposed taxing demands on working memory. Thus, the results of the study_____

16. Which statement most logically completes the sentence?

(A) are only useful for evaluating the effects of exercise on relatively simple cognitive exercises.

(B) might misleadingly suggest differences in cognitive ability between subjects that are not genuine.

(C) should not be interpreted as representative of people not included in the study.

(D) reveal more about humans' abilities to remember trivial details than to remember details that would be relevant in professional or academic settings.

Many museum collectors value works of African art created before many African nations were colonized by Europeans in the late nineteenth century, believing such works to reflect the values of various traditional African cultures. Indeed, despite the diversity of art within the continent, many African cultures' art shared some common traits: for instance, sculptures often functioned as talismans or as intended means of communication with spirits. However, African cultures never existed in a vacuum, and many did interact with European explorers pre-colonization. The Kuba people of the Democratic Republic of Congo, for example, made studded throne chairs that seemingly incorporated European stylistic elements. Thus, many researchers have concluded that

17. Which statement most logically completes the sentence?
    (A) while many African cultures created works of art reflective of their own values and traditions, European influence on African artwork predates colonization of regions of Africa by Europeans.
    (B) many art collectors harbor simplistic views about pre-colonial African art primarily because they are unfamiliar with European artistic traditions.
    (C) any similarities between pre-colonial African art and European art should be attributed to mere happenstance.
    (D) any African artifact with clear signatures of European stylistic influence should be dated to no earlier than the late nineteenth century.

A team of biologists studying the acuteness of mice's sense of smell conducted a study in which they knocked out (removed) the gene *Kv.1.3* from some mice. This mutation causes changes to the olfactory bulb in the brain, involved in processing smell and distinguishing between scents. In the study, wildtype mice and mutant *Kv.1.3*-deleted mice were both about 90% successful locating a food reward in which a peppermint odorant was diluted by a factor of 100. When it was diluted by a factor of 10 billion, wildtype mice had no success in the task and nearly all mutant mice were, suggesting_____

18. Which statement most logically completes the sentence?
    (A) diluting an odorant by a factor of 10 billion is the minimum threshold for weakening mice's ability to discriminate between food odors and background odors.
    (B) declining sensitivity to aromas at different dilution factors is unique to mice and genetically similar rodents.
    (C) wildtype mice decreased expression of *Kv.1.3* as odorants became more dilute.
    (D) expression of *Kv.1.3* diminishes mice's sensitivity to faint smells.

Some evidence from excavations in what is now northwest Alaska suggests that ancient Inuit populations in the Arctic made use of smelted metals that were over 800 years old and that had European origins. But other evidence suggests that Europeans did not arrive in this region until the 1700s. If both the facts about the age and origin of the metals and the estimates of first European contacts in Alaska are correct, this would imply that_____

19. Which finding most logically completes the text?

(A) artifacts from Arctic regions are easier to identify than ones from the past 300 years.

(B) the artifacts likely reached Inuit populations indirectly, such as through trade routes.

(C) a different group of people inhabited ancient Alaska 800 years ago than is conventionally believed.

(D) excavations may have inadvertently damaged metal artifacts from the 1700s.

The Trade-Related Aspects of Intellectual Property Rights (TRIPS) is a global agreement designed to provide a basic framework for protecting intellectual property rights for genetic resources, such as plants. It is supposed to help ensure that those who innovate reap financial rewards while also protecting the public interest in accessing the results of such innovations. While the agreement allows for arrangements for royalty-sharing agreements, there is no legal framework to ensure that benefits from genetic resources are shared fairly. Advocates of farmers' rights worry that the lack of such a framework will result in_____

20. Which statement most logically completes the text?

(A) loss of corporate profits as a result of farmers concealing their discoveries from private companies.

(B) the limitation of studies of genetic materials found on farms from academic institutions and their corporate sponsors.

(C) the preclusion of third parties from ensuring farmers receive adequate compensation for innovations resulting from their knowledge and materials.

(D) farmers failing to refine on agricultural methodologies due to their complacency with inflated subsidies.

The origins of the domestic coconut (*Cocos nucifera*)—an important source of nutrition, fuel, and building materials for many people in tropical climates throughout much of human history—have long been subject to debate, though many scholars believe it was first cultivated in Southeast Asia in the last few thousand years. However, fossil evidence has located what appear to be coconuts from over 60 million years ago in South America—long before early humans existed— and other fossil evidence has shown coconut fossils millions of years old in other regions of the globe. Based on the fossil evidence, evolutionary biologist Kenneth Olsen concluded that_____

21. Which statement most logically completes the text?
    (A) the cultivation of coconuts in South America likely predates its cultivation in Southeast Asia.
    (B) people in Southeast Asia must have acquired a wild form of coconuts from South American people through trade thousands of years ago.
    (C) an ancient form of a coconut underwent a dispersal event that predates humans.
    (D) all modern coconuts likely descend from a single variety that is domesticated, not wild.

Mysterious cave paintings created about 36,000 years ago in France's Chauvet cave have long been subject to anthropological debate. Many scholars believe that these paintings reflect some sort of religious or spiritual purpose, in part since the images of animals depicted were not those typically hunted by humans: perhaps they were intended to magically invoke fertility or power. The discovery in 2016 that a volcanic eruption took place in that region 30,000-40,000 years ago might upend religious interpretations; instead, it may hint that prehistoric people were literally portraying a natural disaster, which could explain the red daubs seen next to animals in the pictures. Because red daubs can also be associated with abstract painting techniques and because the artists left no written record of their culture, however, the red daubs_____

22. Which statement most logically completes the text?
    (A) would be difficult to account for if they did not represent lava from the volcanic eruption.
    (B) cannot conclusively be attributed to the painters' witnessing of the volcanic eruption.
    (C) suggest that most paintings with religious themes contain abstract artistic symbols.
    (D) eliminate the possibility that the painters sought to literally depict their environment.

Many scholars agree that farming methods spread from the Middle East and Mediterranean to Central Europe around 11,000 years ago. Studies of mitochondrial DNA, which is passed on matrilineally, suggest that farmers in the Near East had local European ancestry. Yet studies of Y-chromosomes (transmitted along paternal lines) of modern Europeans and Middle Easterners suggest that these farmers had genetic origins from the Middle East and southeastern Europe. These seemingly contradictory findings can be reconciled if _____

23. Which statement most logically completes the text?

(A) Middle Eastern farmers did not move to Europe in large numbers but instead transmitted their ideas and technologies through trade routes.

(B) female farmers from the Middle East and southern Europe migrated to central Europe in large numbers and started families with males of local European ancestry.

(C) male farmers from the Middle East and southern Europe established farms in central Europe and started families with local female hunter gatherers.

(D) Middle Eastern and southern European families moved to isolated areas of central Europe to establish their own farms, and they did not intermingle with the local population.

A difficulty in studying whether getting promoted to CEO of a large company alters one's behavior lies in ensuring that the experiment has an appropriate control group. In order to determine if a CEO's behavior is changed in a significant way from other workers, researchers must compare CEOs at large companies to comparable people who did not get promoted to CEO. But because researchers cannot control who will get promoted in advance, they_____

24. Which statement most logically completes the text?

(A) will not be able to gather data on how CEOs behave inside and outside professional contexts.

(B) should find control group participants who are significantly different from those typically promoted to CEO.

(C) will likely have difficulty finding appropriate control subjects.

(D) can only study people who already worked as a CEO rather than people who are or will become a CEO in the future.

All domesticated crops have a wildtype ancestor. Researchers have long believed that a single domestication event for corn (maize) happened in Mexico and that after corn was fully domesticated, it spread further South to the Amazon. But a genetic analysis of 5,000-year-old maize by scientists at the Smithsonian National Museum of Natural History found that it included a mixture of genes for domesticated corn and teosinte, which is only found in corn's wild ancestors, suggesting the domestication process was not yet complete. Yet maize was already being cultivated in the Amazon and Europe at least 6.500 years ago, leading the researchers to conclude that _____

25. Which statement most logically completes the text?

(A) corn was cultivated in Europe before it was cultivated in Mexico.

(B) corn was domesticated independently in different regions.

(C) the wildtype ancestor of corn did not originate in Mexico.

(D) Amazonian corn likely descended from a single ancestor that was domesticated.

Unit 2: Craft and Structure

Week 4: Structure and Function

Pre-Lesson Reflection Activity

Suppose your teacher gives you an assignment in which you have to answer one of the following questions in a well-developed essay. Consider the different purposes of each assignment. What would be different about the way you approach each assignment? What would be the same? Which seems more challenging to you, and why?

- Option A: Explain three specific ways artificial intelligence (AI) has changed society.
- Option B: On balance, do you think AI has been more beneficial or detrimental to the welfare of the general population?

You might notice that Option A requires you to write an informative essay. To approach this, you would likely have to do very careful research and present a coherent discussion of specific ways AI has changed society. For example, you might discuss how businesses leverage this technology to tailor their marketing to specific people. Option B will also require you to do research if you wish to write a compelling and well-supported essay. However, this option gives you more freedom to insert your personal opinion and evaluation of the evidence. Your task is not merely to explain but to persuade the reader. While the SAT will not require you to do any research or craft your own arguments, you will need to analyze how the authors you read structure their writings to achieve specific goals.

In **Lesson 1**, we explored **central idea and detail** questions, which focused on identifying what texts were literally saying. What were the big ideas the authors wished to convey? What were smaller details that supported these points?

Function and structure questions, by contrast, focus less on what authors say and more on **how and why** they say it. The author's **purpose** is the author's reason for writing a particular work. For example, an author might compose a poem in order to provide a social commentary on a situation, describe a sight in nature, or convey his feelings for another person. A reporter might write an article on a recent scientific discovery or to comment on its significance.

Suppose you write an open letter to your school district's superintendent's office in your school newspaper arguing for later school start times, citing research about its benefits to students, including studies linking later school start time to improved academic performance, better physical health, and minimized behavior issues. In this case,

- The **main idea** of your article is that there are many benefits to later school start times.
- The **purpose** (function) of your article is to **persuade** your school district to alter its policies surrounding school start times.
- The **structure** of your piece might be a brief introduction summarizing your beliefs and bulleted outline expanding on specific benefits of later school start times.

In the context of the SAT, function and structure questions will be presented in three main ways, but they all generally require the broadly same approach. For all question types, you must do the following:

1) Read the passage carefully.
2) Determine the point the author is making.
3) Reflect on what purpose the details the author makes serve.

When reflecting on the author's purpose, consider the following questions.

1) Is the piece more informative (imparting knowledge on a topic or situation) or persuasive (attempting to convince the reader to adopt a certain view)?
2) Who is the intended audience of the piece?
3) Who is the speaker? Is it a first person narrator describing her own experiences and feelings? Is it an all-knowing narrator? Is it a journalist or scholar reporting on a state of affairs?
4) What is the intended emotional impact of the piece, if any? Is it positive or celebratory in tone? Sad? Neutral? Reflecting on such issues can be especially important for excerpts from poems and fiction passages.

Primary Purpose

Primary purpose questions ask you to identify the main purpose of the text. They are related to **main idea** questions, but their focus is more on the author's goal in writing the text rather than the content of the writing.

The left column of the table below summarizes examples of main ideas (for passages not shown). The right side shows examples of primary purposes that correspond to those main ideas.

Main Idea Example	Corresponding Primary Purpose Examples
Free speech cannot exist in a society in which people feel threatened for speaking their honest opinions.	To argue conditions that are necessary for free speech to exist in society.
Evidence shows that the sweet potato likely originated in South America and spread westward to the Pacific.	To summarize evidence that resolves a scientific inquiry.
The protagonist of a short story struggles with a decision to break the confidence of a friend who is about to do something unethical.	To portray the internal conflict of a central character.

Mini Activity 3

Given a main idea for a text (not shown), speculate a possible main purpose

Main Idea	Purpose
1. The Scientific Revolution encouraged individualism because it showcased the capabilities of the human mind.	
2. An ideal agriculture system borrows elements from both conventional agriculture and organic agriculture.	
3. The genetic complexity of potatoes has traditionally made it difficult for scientists to study their genetic origins.	
4. While Keesha remains calm in stressful situations, her sister Katherine panics.	
5. Scientists were able to use a new machine learning technique to get a clearer picture of a black hole than ever before.	

For the first situation, a possible main purpose might be "to explain how the Scientific Revolution encouraged individualism " or even something more broad like "to explain an effect of the Scientific Revolution."

For the second situation, a possible main purpose might be "to argue what an ideal agricultural system requires."

For the third situation, a possible main purpose is "to explain the challenges inherent in studying the genetic history of potatoes."

For the fourth situation, one possible main purpose is "to contrast characteristics of two sisters."

For the fifth situation, one possible main purpose is "to note the significance of a new methodology."

To approach primary purpose questions, do the following:
1) Read the passage carefully.
2) In your own words, reflect on the main idea or topic of the passage.
3) Consider what broader function that the main idea serves.
4) Read each choice carefully, eliminating any that present inaccuracies or more minor details from the text. The right answer should be broad enough in scope to capture the essence of the paragraph but specific enough as to not be vague, or unclear.

Sample 1

The excerpt below is from *Mansfield Park* by Jane Austen.

To the education of her daughters Lady Bertram paid not the smallest attention. She had not time for such cares. She was a woman who spent her days in sitting, nicely dressed, on a sofa, doing some long piece of needlework, of little use and no beauty, thinking more of her pug than her children, but very indulgent to the latter when it did not put herself to inconvenience, guided in everything important by Sir Thomas, and in smaller concerns by her sister. Had she possessed greater leisure for the service of her girls, she would probably have supposed it unnecessary, for they were under the care of a governess, with proper masters, and could want nothing more.

What is the primary purpose of the text?
  A) To convey Lady Bertram's inattention to her daughters' educational endeavors.
  B) To underscore that Lady Bertram's daughters have a deeper respect for their governess than for their mother.
  C) To recount events in Lady Bertram's life that led her to develop a blasé attitude toward the education sector.
  D) To describe how the luxuriousness of Lady Bertram's surroundings causes her to feel complacent about her daughters' educational progress.

The text focuses on Lady Bertram and describes how little attention she pays to her daughters' education. She seemed to concern herself more with superficial and materialistic affairs. She did not feel the need to put too much focus on her girls' needs, as they were under the care of capable individuals, such as the governess. Overall, the main idea seems to be that Lady Bertram paid little attention to her girls' educations and was more concerned with her own leisure. While there are several potential ways to phrase the primary purpose of this text, a reasonable prediction might be that the main purpose is to convey Lady Bertram's lack of concern for her daughters' education or her lack of involvement in tending to their needs.

Choice A seems like a logical choice. The paragraph makes clear from the outset that Lady Bertram paid little attention to her daughters' education, and the rest of the paragraph expands on this idea. She did not want to give her children any extra attention that would detract from her leisure and seemed to trust that they were in good hands. **This is the correct choice.**

Choice B is not supported by the text. While it might be a reasonable supposition, more information is needed to know if this is true. All we learn is that Lady Bertram seems to think the governess meets her daughters' needs, but we learn nothing about her daughters' opinions.

Choice C is beyond the scope of the passage. We do not learn about events in Lady Bertram's life that might explain her attitude toward the education sector. Also, the paragraph does not discuss the education sector in general.

Choice D is not correct because although Lady Bertram seems to be complacent about her daughters' educational situation, there is not an explanation about how this complacency is caused by the luxuriousness of her surroundings. The passage also does not indicate how luxurious Lady Bertram's surroundings are.

Sample 2

Most astronomers believe gas giant planets like Jupiter can only form around stars that are large enough to provide the planet with enough rocky materials to accrete together to form the planet's core. A large gas giant called T0I-5205 shocked scientists when it was found around a small red dwarf star. Based on current theoretical models for how gas giants form, the star would not have enough rocky material to support the creation of a gas giant of TOI-5205's size. Lead author of the study Shubham Kanodia stated that this "forbidden" planet never should have existed and stretches our understanding about what we know about how gas giants are born.

What is the primary purpose of the passage?
   A) To describe how a planet formed around a star that would typically be too small to support that planet's existence.
   B) To announce an astronomical finding that challenges conventional understanding about conditions that constrain gas giant formation.
   C) To explain why red dwarfs lack sufficient rocky material to serve as viable host stars to planets comparable in size to TOI-525.
   D) To clarify why a discovery that seems to violate established theoretical models can be reconciled with evidence from experimental studies.

The main idea is that TO1-5205 is a gas giant planet that is larger than theoretical models of planet formation would predict is possible given the size of its star. Thus, the purpose is to recount a surprise discovery that challenges theoretical models about how gas giants form.

Choice A is incorrect because it is not known how the planet described in the passage formed around its star.

Choice B is correct. The passage does announce an astronomical finding (the discovery of TOI-525 around a red dwarf) that challenges a conventional understanding about gas giant formation (based on conventional understandings, the planet should never have been formed).

Choice C is a trap. Though it is briefly mentioned that red dwarfs do not have enough rocky material to be a host star for planets of the size of TO1-525 according to conventional models, it does not go into detail about why. The fact that TOI-525 exists shows that it is possible for a planet of that size to have a red dwarf as its star. Also, C does not mention the key idea that there was a discovery of a planet that challenges conventional thinking about how planets form.

Choice D is wrong because there is no discussion of how the finding can be reconciled (made consistent with) findings from other studies.

Function

While primary purpose questions ask you to identify the main purpose of the passage as a whole, function questions will ask you for the function of a specific excerpt from a passage, generally a sentence.

Below are some of the most common functions (this list is not exhaustive).
1) Comparisons: show similarity between people, things, ideas, and events.
   - Example: "Penguins and ostriches are both flightless birds."

2) Contrast: show differences between people, things, ideas, and events.
   - Example: "While Xiomara is quiet and reserved, her sister is loud and outgoing."

3) Cause and effect: shows how one person, thing, idea, or event results from another.
   - Example: "The lack of rain in the region led to crop failures."

4) Sequence: shows the order in which events happen.
   - Example: "Light microscopes were used to examine biological structures in the 1600s. In the 1900s, a microscope that uses electrons instead of light was developed."

5) Support: evidence that an idea is correct or a circumstance is true.
   - Example: "The experiment provided evidence supporting the hypothesis that musical ability helps one learn a foreign language."

6) Expansion: builds on viewpoint held or evidence already existing (note that the underlined portion of the example below shows the example of providing expansion).

  - Example: "Heinrich Hertz discovered the photoelectric effect, the release of electrons that occurs when a beam of light is shined on metal. Max Planck continued studies on the photoelectric effect and found that the number of electrons released was proportional to the frequency of the light."

7) Contradiction: evidence that an idea is not correct or a circumstance is not true.

  - Example: "Copernicus's studies of the stars led him to believe that the Earth revolved around the sun, contradicting the Aristotelian model, which stated that the sun revolved around the Earth."

8) Modification: a finding or piece of evidence that revises or corrects a view that was previously held (note that the underlined portion of the example below shows the example of modification).

  - Example: "Rutherford showed that the atom consisted of a positive center surrounded by negative electrons. Bohr revised this model to show that electrons are not in a diffuse cloud, but in energy levels known as orbitals."

9) Context: background information that clarifies the significance of other information mentioned previously or after (note that the underlined portion of the example below shows the example of providing context).

  - Example: "Because Lulu was always used to getting her way at home, she had difficulty adjusting to her school where teachers did not cater to her whims."

Tip: Pay attention to important **transition words** that signal certain relationships. These can often provide useful clues to determining the function of a sentence in a text. The chart below gives some examples of common transition words that highlight different relationships (note that this is not an exhaustive list).

Comparison	Contrast	Cause and Effect	Sequence	Support	Contradiction
Like	Unlike	Consequently	First	Confirms	Opposes
As	Conversely	Because	Then	Proves	Contradicts
Similarly	However	Thus	Next	Evidence	Disproves
	Nevertheless	Therefore	Last	Corroborates	Discredits
	Nonetheless	As a result			
	In contrast				

To approach function questions, do the following:

1) Read the passage carefully, reflecting on the main idea and primary purpose.
2) In your own words, identify what the underlined sentence or excerpt literally tells you.
3) Reflect on how the underlined sentence relates to the surrounding sentences and predict its general function.
4) Read each choice carefully, eliminating any that present an inaccurate characterization of the sentence. Beware of choices that better describe other sentences in the text besides the one being tested.

Sample 3

Argentine ants have outcompeted native ants for food in part due to their aggression and willingness to take risks. Researchers from UCLA believed these ants would forage when they were starving because they had more to lose and everything to gain, leading starving ants to act more aggressively than satiated ants to obtain food in high-risk environments. The research team used formic acid to give ants the impression that they were in a high-risk environment with competitors. Lead researcher Bryce Barbee was surprised to find that well-fed ants were more likely to take risks while starving ants were more cautious in their foraging in high-risk scenarios, though starving ants did forage more aggressively in low-risk scenarios. The team speculated that well-fed ants are more likely to take risks when foraging under high-risk conditions because they are more likely to have the strength to survive threats they encounter, showing the importance of energy costs in foraging decisions.

Which choice best describes the function of the underlined sentence in the text as a whole?
   A) It provides the rationale for examining a research question.
   B) It provides context for why a certain experimental finding puzzled researchers.
   C) It details a procedure that allowed for the creation of an experimental condition.
   D) It highlights a methodological flaw that led to a counterintuitive analysis.

The passage describes a study that led to a counterintuitive finding. The underlined sentence itself presents part of the experiment's procedure, namely how conditions of "high risk" were mimicked in a laboratory setting.

Choice A is incorrect because the sentence does not present the rationale, or reason, a research question was examined. It instead describes a procedure done to carry out a study.

Choice B is incorrect because the sentence does not provide context, or background information, about why a finding was surprising. If anything, the sentence before the underlined one comes closest to achieving this goal, as it notes why researchers expected starving ants to be more aggressive in high-risk situations.

Choice C is literally true and matches our prediction. It notes a component of the procedure needed to produce a certain condition: the formic acid was used to make ants perceive they were in a high-risk environment. **This is the correct choice.**

Choice D is incorrect because although the finding was counterintuitive to researchers (opposite of what they expected based on logic), there is no suggestion that a flaw, or problem, in the study contributed to this result.

Sample 4

The excerpt below is adapted from "The Gray Man" by Sarah Orne Jewett.

An instinctive curiosity and alarm possessed the country men and women about the newcomer for a while, but soon faded out and disappeared. The newcomer was by no means a hermit; he tried to be friendly, and inclined toward a certain kindliness and familiarity. He bought a comfortable store of winter provisions from his new acquaintants, giving everyone his price, and spoke more at length, as time went on, of current events, of politics and the weather, and the town's own news and concerns. There was a sober cheerfulness about the man, as if he had known trouble and perplexity, and was fulfilling some mission that gave him pain; yet he saw some gain and reward beyond; therefore he could be contented with his life and such strange surroundings. He was more and more eager to form brotherly relations with the farmers near his home. There was almost a pleading look in his kind face at times, as if he feared the later prejudice of his associates.

Which choice best describes the function of the underlined sentence in the text as a whole?
   A) It provides context that sets up a description of a character's efforts to bond with his neighbors.
   B) It dispels a common misconception that many of a character's neighbors had about him.
   C) It introduces the setting in which a significant event will take place.
   D) It elaborates on the previous sentence's description of a character.

We learn in this sentence that the newcomer made efforts to be friendly. The following sentences go into more detail about this: be bought stuff from them at their asking price, talked to them more, and was eager to form brotherly relations.

Choice A is correct because it provides context that sets up a description of the man's attempts to bond with his neighbors. We learn he tried to be friendly and was not a hermit (recluse), and the next sentence tells us the specific efforts he made to connect with his neighbors.

Choice B is incorrect because while it does dispel a potential misconception the reader might have about the newcomer (by clarifying that he is not a hermit), it does not indicate that most of his neighbors believed this about him. All we know is that their initial curiosity about him wore off, and this was discussed in the previous sentence.

Choice C is incorrect because the focus is on the character, not the setting. It is unclear what significant event this choice is referencing.

Choice D is incorrect because the sentence provides new information about the newcomer. It does not elaborate (provide more details) about a description. Rather, the third sentence elaborates on information provided about the character in the underlined sentence.

Overall Structure

On occasion, a question might ask for the **overall structure** of the passage. Approach these much as you would function questions, but consider the passage **as a whole** rather than one underlined portion.

Sample 5

The excerpt below is adapted from "The Corn Husker" by Emily Pauline Johnson.

> Hard by the Indian lodges, where the bush
> Breaks in a clearing, through ill-fashioned fields,
> She comes to labor, when the first still hush
> Of autumn follows large and recent yields.
> Age in her fingers, hunger in her face,
> Her shoulders stooped with weight of work and years,
> But rich in tawny coloring of her race,
> She comes a-field to strip the purple ears.
> And all her thoughts are with the days gone by,
> Ere might's injustice banished from their lands
> Her people, that to-day unheeded lie,
> Like the dead husks that rustle through her hands.

Which of the following best describes the overall structure of the text?
A) It sketches the autobiography of a woman and then contrasts her lived experiences to those of other people from her culture.
B) It explains how a woman was forced into agricultural labor and then alludes to her plans to seek justice against those responsible for her suffering.
C) It provides a vivid description that conveys a woman's hardships and then compares her people to a crop she is handling.
D) It highlights a similarity between a woman's place of residence and place of work and then highlights how her handling of the corn husks brings her closer to nature.

The beginning of the poem provides a description of an old Indian woman hard at work in the fields. We are given the impression that she has faced hardships. For example, she appears hungry and her shoulders are stooped by the weight of her labor over the years. We learn that her people have unjustly been banished from their lands. At the end, her people (Indians) are compared to the dead corn husks they handle in the fields, dramatizing the injustices they have faced.

Choice A is not technically correct. While it provides a description of a woman, it does not give her autobiography (life story). The end of the poem also does not contrast (show differences) between her experiences and those of other people.

Choice B is wrong because the passage does not explain in detail how the woman was forced into labor. More importantly, there are no discussions of her plans to seek injustice. We just know she experienced injustice.

Choice C is correct. We do get a vivid (detailed) description of the woman: her appearance, her struggles, and her thoughts. At the end, her people are compared to dead corn husks.

Choice D is wrong because though an Indian lodge is mentioned, the passage does not detail similarities between the woman's home and place of work. While the woman is handling corn, the tone is somber. We don't get the sense that she feels closer to nature.

Sample 6

The excerpt below is from NASA's article, "Reflections on the Scientific and Cultural Implications of Finding Life in the Cosmos" by Neil deGrasse Tyson.

Ordinarily, there is no riskier step that a scientist (or anyone) can take than to make sweeping generalizations from just one example. At the moment, life on Earth is the only known life in the universe, but there are compelling arguments to suggest we are not alone. Indeed, most astrophysicists accept a high probability of there being life elsewhere in the universe, if not on other planets or on moons within our own solar system. The numbers are, well, astronomical: If the count of planets in our solar system is not unusual, then there are more planets in the universe than the sum of all sounds and words ever uttered by every human who has ever lived. To declare that Earth must be the only planet in the cosmos with life would be inexcusably egocentric of us.

Which of the following best describes the overall structure of the text?
   A) It highlights a common risk scientists face and then details ways they can overcome that risk.
   B) It describes a common belief amongst a class of professionals and then shows why that belief is likely mistaken.
   C) It presents a claim with which the author agrees and then explains his reasoning for supporting that argument.
   D) It acknowledges a lack of evidence for a particular contention and then recommends research methods that can be used to locate such evidence.

Tyson makes the claim that there are compelling (convincing) arguments to suggest Earth isn't the only place with life in the universe. He elaborates on why he believes this is so. Based on sheer probability alone, he thinks it is mathematically unlikely there are no other planets with life in the universe.

Choice A is wrong because although the passage mentions that it is generally risky to make broad generalizations, it does not discuss a common risk scientists make or ways to overcome that risk.

Choice B is wrong because although the passage presents a common belief held by scientists (that there is likely life on other planets), Tyson agrees with this view.

Choice C is correct. Tyson presents the claim that there is likely life on other planets and explains his reasoning for thinking this.

Choice D is wrong because although Tyson acknowledges evidence of life on other planets has not yet been found, he does not propose a solution for addressing this.

Drill 4

The excerpt below is from "For Love of the Hills" by Susan Glaspell. The main character has recently moved from Denver to Chicago.

It was hard to hold back the tears as she dwelt upon the fact that it was very little she had asked of Chicago. She had asked only for a chance to do the work for which she was trained, in order that she might go to the art classes at night. She had read in the papers of that mighty young city of the Middle West—the heart of the continent—of its brawn and its brain and its grit. She had supposed that Chicago, of all places, would appreciate what she wanted to do. The day she drew her hard-earned one hundred dollars from the bank in Denver—how the sun had shone that day in Denver, how clear the sky had been, and how bracing the air!—she had quite taken it for granted that her future was assured. And now, after tasting for three weeks the cruelty of indifference, she looked back to those visions with a hard little smile.

1. What is the main purpose of the text?

   (A) To explain why a protagonist plans on moving back to her hometown.

   (B) To show that the narrator plans to parlay the skills from her art classes into a new career that gives her more fulfillment.

   (C) To suggest the difficulty that the protagonist has experienced in adjusting to her new life circumstances.

   (D) To explain why Chicago will never be able to meet the protagonist's emotional needs.

Some of the most important discoveries resulted from fortunate accidents. In 1928, Scottish physician-scientist Alexander Fleming had been conducting a series of experiments on a common staphylococcal bacteria, associated with staph infections. Upon returning from a vacation, he noticed a strange mold growing in one of the uncovered petri dishes that seemed to be killing the surrounding bacteria. He isolated and studied this mold, leading him to discover that the mold produced penicillin, an antibacterial agent that has since gone on to be used to save millions of lives of people suffering from bacterial infections.

2. Which choice best states the main purpose of this text?

   (A) To explain how penicillin works to combat bacterial infections.

   (B) To draw attention to Alexander Fleming's research on staphylococcal bacteria.

   (C) To discuss Alexander's Fleming's discovery of penicillin.

   (D) To indicate how accessible penicillin is on a global scale.

The Obsidian Cliff is a mountain of black glass in Yellowstone National Park. For thousands of years, stones from this cliff have been used to fashion a variety of tools. Yale researchers recently applied X-ray fluorescence technology to analyze the origins of some tools over 10,000 years old collected from this region that are now on display at the Peabody Museum. While the tools were originally thought to have two origin points in Iran, the analysis revealed seven points of origin, highlighting the complexity of early humans' social networks. <u>Although X-ray technology can reveal the source of the obsidian artifacts, it cannot show us how these artifacts arrived at Yellowstone in the first place.</u>

3. Which choice best describes the function of the underlined sentence in the overall structure of the text?

   (A) It explains how X-ray fluorescence is able to ascertain the origin of certain artifacts.
   (B) It highlights a limitation in the capabilities of a research technique.
   (C) It critiques scientists for failing to consider factors that influenced their findings.
   (D) It encourages other researchers to conduct a new study that resolves a mystery.

The poem below is "Changing is Not Vanishing" by Carlos Montezuma

Who says the Indian race is vanishing?
The Indians will not vanish.
The feathers, paint and moccasin will vanish, but the Indians,—never!
Just as long as there is a drop of human blood in America, the Indians will not
    vanish.
His spirit is everywhere; the American Indian will not vanish.
He has changed externally but he has not vanished.
He is an industrial and commercial man, competing with the world; he has not
    vanished.
Wherever you see an Indian upholding the standard of his race, there you see
    the Indian man—he has not vanished.
The man part of the Indian is here, there and everywhere.
The Indian race vanishing? No, never! The race will live on and prosper forever.

4. Which choice best states the main purpose of this text?

   (A) To consider how undergoing personal transformations can be both rewarding and self-effacing
   (B) To question whether a group of people can maintain a commitment to their traditional values while adopting new customs.
   (C) To argue that people's actions in their personal lives are more important than their actions in their professional lives.
   (D) To refute the notion that a shift in outward behavior patterns of a group of people is indicative of the disappearance of that group.

The poem below is "Tenebris" by Angelina Weld Grimke.

There is a tree, by day,
That, at night, Has a shadow,
A hand huge and black,
With fingers long and black.
All through the dark,
Against the white man's house,
In the little wind,
The black hand plucks and plucks
At the bricks.
The bricks are the color of blood
and very small.
Is it a black hand,
Or is it a shadow?

5. Which choice best describes the overall structure of the text?

   (A) It describes a distinctive sight and then ponders what meaning to attribute to that sight.
   (B) It explains how a scene in nature parallels a societal conflict and then questions how this conflict can be rectified.
   (C) It portrays an outdoor scene as quiet yet eerie and then notes how that scene impacts the speaker's emotional state.
   (D) It examines how a synthetic structure is impacted by a natural one and then expresses skepticism about the speaker's analysis.

Plants native to Hawaii like the pukiawe (*Leptecophylla tameiameiae*) depend on birds for survival, as they help facilitate seed dispersal. Unfortunately, many native species of birds have gone extinct. But non-native bird species can often fulfill the ecological niche of native birds, helping native plants thrive. Researchers led by Jeferson Vizentin-Bugoni began monitoring seed dispersal networks in Hawaii, where many alien bird species have replaced native ones. They found that alien bird species like the red vented bulbul (*Pyconotus cafer*), native to Asia, functioned as a main disperser of the seeds of native Hawaiian plants.

6. Which choice best describes the function of the third sentence in the overall structure of the text?

   (A) It presents a generalization that is later exemplified by the example of the red vented bulbul.
   (B) It offers an alternative explanation to a finding by Vizentin-Bugoni and colleagues.
   (C) It presents a hypothesis that Vizentin-Bugoni designed an experiment to test.
   (D) It provides context that clarifies why the red vented bulbul spread to new locations.

The poem below is "O me! O life!" by Walt Whitman.

Oh me! Oh life! of the questions of these recurring,
Of the endless trains of the faithless, of cities fill'd with the foolish,
Of myself forever reproaching myself, (for who more foolish than I, and who more faithless?)
Of eyes that vainly crave the light, of the objects mean, of the struggle ever renew'd,
Of the poor results of all, of the plodding and sordid crowds I see around me,
Of the empty and useless years of the rest, with the rest me intertwined,
The question, O me! so sad, recurring—What good amid these, O me, O life?

Answer.
That you are here—that life exists and identity,
That the powerful play goes on, and you may contribute a verse.

7. Which choice best describes the overall structure of the text?
    (A) The speaker expresses an increasingly prevalent belief about the corruption of society and then explains what led him to change his perspective.
    (B) The speaker laments flaws that he sees in society and in himself and then asserts his worth to society.
    (C) The speaker expresses consternation about not knowing his own place in the world and then makes peace with not understanding his value.
    (D) The speaker addresses a criticism that others have waged against him and then announces that he is no longer bothered by such critiques.

The excerpt below is from Jane Austen's novel *Mansfield Park*. The speaker is Thomas Bertram, who is discussing with his wife the prospect of taking in their niece, Fanny, to live with them and their children.

"Should her disposition be really bad," said Sir Thomas, "we must not, for our own children's sake, continue her in the family; but there is no reason to expect so great an evil. We shall probably see much to wish altered in her, and must prepare ourselves for gross ignorance, some meanness of opinions, and very distressing vulgarity of manner; but these are not incurable faults; nor, I trust, can they be dangerous for her associates. Had my daughters been *younger* than herself, I should have considered the introduction of such a companion as a matter of very serious moment; but, as it is, I hope there can be nothing to fear for *them*, and everything to hope for *her*, from the association."

8. Which choice best states the main purpose of this text?
    (A) To elaborate on the idea that Fanny lacks the requisite skills needed to flourish in elite society.
    (B) To lament that Fanny's lack of refined manners will be a great inconvenience to Thomas and his wife.
    (C) To demonstrate Thomas's assurance that the introduction of Fanny into the family household is unlikely to have a corrupting effect on his other children.
    (D) To assert that Thomas has come up with a comprehensive plan to successfully correct the faults he believes exist in Fanny's character and manners.

The poem below is "America" by Claude Mckay.

Although she feeds me bread of bitterness,
And sinks into my throat her tiger's tooth,
Stealing my breath of life, I will confess
I love this cultured hell that tests my youth!
Her vigor flows like tides into my blood,
Giving me strength erect against her hate.
Her bigness sweeps my being like a flood.
Yet as a rebel fronts a king in state,
I stand within her walls with not a shred
Of terror, malice, not a word of jeer.
Darkly I gaze into the days ahead,
And see her might and granite wonders there,
Beneath the touch of Time's unerring hand,
Like priceless treasures sinking in the sand.

9. Which choice best states the main purpose of this text?
    (A) To simultaneously critique and express admiration for the characteristics of a country that leave an impression on the speaker.
    (B) To suggest that a country's energetic pace of daily life mitigates its culpability for its unjust practices.
    (C) To express despair for the future of a country despite its tendency to invigorate its residents by testing them.
    (D) To describe how people from diverse cultural backgrounds are differentially impacted by a nation's attributes.

A lichen is a complex life form that includes a symbiotic relationship between a fungus and an alga. Scientists have long been puzzled by why some seemingly closely related lichens produce toxins that are harmful to mammals and other do not. A team of scientists from Helsinki led by Leena Myllys conducted a genomic analysis of lichens in their toxic and non-toxic forms and could not find a genetic difference between the two. This led the team to conclude that DNA analysis was not adequate for explaining why some lichens develop toxic properties.

10. Which choice best describes the function of the second sentence in the overall structure of the text?
    (A) It presents the central finding of Myllys's team's study.
    (B) It acknowledges a point of contention between Myllys's team and the broader scientific community.
    (C) It notes a mystery that Myllys's team attempted and failed to solve.
    (D) It describes an innovative methodology employed in Myllys's study.

The excerpt below is adapted from "A White Heron" by Sarah Orne Jewett

The companions followed the shady wood–road, the cow taking slow steps and the child very fast ones. The cow stopped long at the brook to drink, as if the pasture were not half a swamp, and Sylvia stood still and waited, letting her bare feet cool themselves in the shoal water, while the great twilight moths struck softly against her. She waded on through the brook as the cow moved away, and listened to the thrushes with a heart that beat fast with pleasure. There was a stirring in the great boughs overhead. They were full of little birds and beasts that seemed to be wide awake, and going about their world, or else saying good–night to each other in sleepy twitters. Sylvia herself felt sleepy as she walked along. However, it was not much farther to the house, and the air was soft and sweet. She was not often in the woods so late as this, and it made her feel as if she were a part of the gray shadows and the moving leaves.

11. Which choice best states the main purpose of the text?

(A) To contrast the stillness of the woodlands with the bustle of farm life.

(B) To portray the setting as a character and her cow walk home.

(C) To describe how a character has become more adventurous over time.

(D) To highlight a character's uneasiness in her surroundings.

Theodora Skipitares is a theater director, but she is also a visual artist who uses realistic life-sized puppets as well as miniature ones in many of her works to illuminate human and social issues. Her work *The Age Of Invention* tells the story of three centuries worth of American inventions using over 300 puppets, which help convey social messages, such as a commentary on the plights of pioneer women. The performance is adapted from the seventeenth century Japanese tradition of Bunraku theater, which makes use of puppets, text, and music. The performance sheds insight into Skipitares's deep connection with the Bunraku tradition, which she admires for the tension it produces in striking a balance between realism and non-realism to convey important themes.

12. Which choice best describes the overall structure of the passage?

(A) It makes a claim about an artist and then supports that claim with an example.

(B) It describes how a tradition has influenced an artist and how the artist has altered elements of it to appeal to modern audiences.

(C) It describes the puppets used in *The Age of Invention* and then explains how they relate to the Bunraku tradition.

(D) It describes a similarity between a typical seventeenth-century performance and a particular modern one and then notes a subtle distinction between them.

The excerpt below is from the poem "If—" by Rudyard Kipling. In the poem, the speaker is addressing his son.

If you can talk with crowds and keep your virtue,
   Or walk with Kings—nor lose the common touch,
If neither foes nor loving friends can hurt you,
   If all men count with you, but none too much;
If you can fill the unforgiving minute
   With sixty seconds' worth of distance run,
Yours is the Earth and everything that's in it,
   And—which is more—you'll be a Man, my son!

13. Which choice best states the main purpose of the text?

(A) To express hope that a child will accomplish more than his parents.

(B) To warn a child about the burdens he will carry in adulthood.

(C) To provide guidance to a child about how to navigate life.

(D) To encourage a child to forcefully assert his authority over others.

The excerpt below is adapted from *O Pioneers!* by Willa Cather.

In eleven long years John Bergson had made but little impression upon the wild land he had come to tame. <u>It was still a wild thing that had its ugly moods</u>; and no one knew when they were likely to come, or why. Mischance hung over it. Its Genius was unfriendly to man. He knew every ridge and draw and gully between him and the horizon. To the south, his plowed fields; to the east, the sod stables, the cattle corral, the pond,—and then the grass. Bergson went over in his mind the things that had held him back. One winter his cattle had perished in a blizzard. The next summer one of his plow horses broke its leg in a prairie dog hole and had to be shot. Another summer he lost his hogs from cholera, and a valuable stallion died from a rattlesnake bite. Time and again his crops had failed.

14. Which choice best describes the function of the underlined excerpt in the text as a whole?

(A) It provides a description of the land that suggests challenges it presents for a character.

(B) It reveals how the natural environment alters the agricultural strategy of humans.

(C) It highlights the beneficial relationship between people and farmland.

(D) It portrays the volatile personality traits of a farmer who tends to his land.

The excerpt below is from *A Gentleman in Moscow* by Amos Towers.

And the waiters? Like those of a Parisian café, the Piazza's waiters could best be complimented as "efficient." Accustomed to navigating crowds, they could easily seat your party of eight at a table for four. Having noted your preferences over the sound of the orchestra, within minutes they would return with the various drinks balanced on a tray and dispense them round the table in rapid succession without misplacing a glass. If, with your menu in hand, you hesitated for even a second to place your order, they would lean over your shoulder and poke at a specialty of the house. And when the last morsel of dessert had been savored, they would whisk away your plate, present your check, and make your change in under a minute. In other words, the waiters of the Piazza knew their trade to the crumb, the spoon, and the kopek.

15. Which choice best describes the function of the underlined sentence in the text as a whole?

(A) It makes a claim that is proven in the following sentence.

(B) It establishes a conflict faced by certain characters the narrator describes.

(C) It provides vivid imagery that establishes a prominent physical setting.

(D) It illustrates an idea that is introduced in the preceding sentence.

The excerpt below is from William Wordsworth's poem "The Stars are Mansions Built by Nature's Hands."

The stars are mansions built by Nature's hand,
And, haply, there the spirits of the blest
Dwell, clothed in radiance, their immortal vest;
Huge Ocean shows, within his yellow strand,
A habitation marvelously planned,
For life to occupy in love and rest;
All that we see--is dome, or vault, or nest,
Or fortress, reared at Nature's sage command.

16. Which choice best describes the overall structure of the text?

(A) It provides a literal description of how a celestial body is formed.

(B) It presents an extended comparison between stars and physical constructions.

(C) It sketches an image of a star and then an image of a luxurious home.

(D) It portrays how stars guide humans in spiritual journeys.

A study by a team of researchers including Adam Heller suggests that exposure to different physical locations can lead to increased happiness. <u>Using GPS tracking from the cellphones of 122 individuals in New York City and Miami over a period of 3 to 4 months, researchers quantified each individual's level of exploration each day— a phenomenon known as roaming entropy; the researchers analyzed how individuals' roaming entropy correlated with self-reported emotions.</u> They found that individuals tended to report more positive emotions on days where they experienced more variety in their physical locations. Thus, experiential diversity may be related to happiness.

17. Which choice best describes the function of the underlined sentence in the text as a whole?

(A) To summarize the findings of the research team's analysis.

(B) To provide details about the research team's methodology.

(C) To note challenges encountered by a team of researchers during data collection and analysis.

(D) To explain the rationale that motivated the team's research question.

The excerpt below is from *The Turn of the Screw* by Henry James. The narrator worked at Bly, a country home in Essex, as a governess looking after two children.

I have not seen Bly since the day I left it, and I daresay that to my older and more informed eyes it would now appear sufficiently contracted. But as my little conductress, with her hair of gold and her frock of blue, danced before me round corners and pattered down passages, I had the view of a castle of romance inhabited by a rosy sprite, such a place as would somehow, for diversion of the young idea, take all color out of storybooks and fairytales. Wasn't it just a storybook over which I had fallen adoze and adream? No; it was a big, ugly, antique, but convenient house, embodying a few features of a building still older, half-replaced and half-utilized, in which I had the fancy of our being almost as lost as a handful of passengers in a great drifting ship. Well, I was, strangely, at the helm!

18. Which choice best states the main purpose of the text?

(A) To explain circumstances that led the narrator to terminate her employment.

(B) To demonstrate that the narrator harbors conflicted feelings about a home that once had strong sentimental value to her.

(C) To convey a contrast between the narrator's past fondness of and present distaste of a location.

(D) To describe the narrator's determination to forget about a troubling time in her past.

The excerpt below is from "Ode to Ethiopia" by Paul Laurence Dunbar.

Thou hast the right to noble pride,
Whose spotless robes were purified
By blood's severe baptism.
Upon thy brow the cross was laid,
And labour's painful sweat-beads made
A consecrating chrism.

No other race, or white or black,
When bound as thou wert, to the rack,
So seldom stooped to grieving;
No other race, when free again,
Forgot the past and proved them men
So noble in forgiving.

Go on and up! Our souls and eyes
Shall follow thy continuous rise;
Our ears shall list thy story
From bards who from thy root shall spring,
and proudly tune their lyres to sing
Of Ethiopia's glory.

19. What is the central purpose of the text?
   (A) To celebrate the character and accomplishment of a group of people who experienced past hardships.
   (B) To advocate for retribution against a class of persons responsible for an injustice against the subjects of the text.
   (C) To detail the horrors of a crushing political system that caused rifts between different cultural groups.
   (D) To advocate for a reconciliation between perpetrators and victims of a previous violation of human rights.

Native American women played an often overlooked role in the women's suffrage movement of the late nineteenth century, which typically centered white middle class women. At the time, women were advocating for equal voting rights and political rights. Many Native women's experience enjoying full political rights within their own tribes and conducting elections uniquely positioned them to influence non-Native suffragist activists: activists such as Elizabeth Cady Stanton and Lucretia Mott were inspired by their visits to Native American communities in which women wielded great political power, thus influencing aspects of their own platforms in the fight for women's rights throughout the United States. Thus, the ideals in Native American societies permeated into the American political system.

20. Which choice best describes the function of the underlined text in the passage as a whole?

   (A) It elaborates on a claim about the political structure within a particular Native American society discussed in the text.

   (B) It offers examples that illustrate a historical trend mentioned in the passage.

   (C) It notes an exception to discussions of the extent of Native women's political activism mentioned later in the passage.

   (D) It provides further details about the political responsibilities of Native women discussed earlier in the text.

Not all animals send accurate information about themselves to other animals. Instead, they often engage in dishonest signaling in order to reap a certain benefit. Fiddler crabs rely on their large claws for fighting; although this claw can be regrown if it is lost in a fight, the new claw is not as strong as the original, though it is similar in appearance. Male fiddler crabs with the weaker regrown claws will often flaunt them in an attempt to ward off potential male attackers. Researchers have found that many would-be attackers are just as deterred from fighting male fiddler crabs who flaunt the regrown large claws as they are from male fiddler crabs who display the stronger, original large claws.

21. Which choice best describes the function of the underlined excerpt in the text as a whole?

   (A) It introduces a physical feature of male fiddler crabs that the rest of the paragraph discusses.

   (B) It explains how potential aggressors react to male fiddler crabs who display their regrown claws.

   (C) It offers a detail about how male fiddler crabs carry out a behavior discussed in the text.

   (D) It describes the appearance of a feature of male fiddler crabs introduced earlier in the text.

The excerpt below is from *Moby Dick* by Herman Melville.

Some years ago — never mind how long precisely — having little or no money in my purse, and nothing particular to interest me on shore, I thought I would sail about a little and see the watery part of the world. It is a way I have of driving off the spleen, and regulating the circulation. Whenever I find myself growing grim about the mouth; whenever it is a damp, drizzly November in my soul; whenever I find myself involuntarily pausing before coffin warehouses, and bringing up the rear of every funeral I meet; <u>and especially whenever my hypos get such an upper hand of me, that it requires a strong moral principle to prevent me from deliberately stepping into the street, and methodically knocking people's hats off — then, I account it high time to get to sea as soon as I can.</u> This is my substitute for pistol and ball. With a philosophical flourish Cato throws himself upon his sword; I quietly take to the ship.

22. Which choice best describes the function of the underlined text in the passage as a whole?

(A) It underscores the narrator's desire to have new experiences beyond the shore.

(B) It provides an extended description of the destination the narrator wishes to reach.

(C) It suggests that the narrator has a more violent imagination than other sailors.

(D) It illustrates why the narrator has had a long fascination with the sea.

The passage below is adapted from *White Fang* by Jack London. White Fang is a wolfdog, and Weedon Scott is his new owner.

Weedon Scott had set himself the task of redeeming White Fang—or rather, of redeeming mankind from the wrong it had done White. So he went out of his way to be especially kind to the Fighting Wolf. Each day he made it a point to caress and pet White Fang, and to do it at length. At first suspicious and hostile, White Fang grew to like this petting. But there was one thing that he never outgrew—his growling. Growl he would, from the moment the petting began till it ended. But it was a growl with a new note in it. A stranger could not hear this note, and to such a stranger the growling of White Fang was an exhibition of primordial savagery, nerve-racking and blood-curdling. But White Fang's throat had become harsh-fibred from the making of ferocious sounds through the many years since his first little rasp of anger in the lair of his cubhood, and he could not soften the sounds of that throat now to express the gentleness he felt. <u>Nevertheless, Weedon Scott's ear and sympathy were fine enough to catch the new note all but drowned in the fierceness—the note that was the faintest hint of a croon of content and that none but he could hear.</u>

23. Which choice best describes the function of the underlined text in the passage as a whole?

(A) It shows that Weedon reacts to White Fang's behavior similarly to other people who witness their interaction.

(B) It hints at the growing emotional bond between White Fang and Weedon.

(C) It explains what White Fang most admires about his new owner.

(D) It vividly describes the distinctive aspects of the sound White Fang makes that allude to his emotional state.

Many educators believe instruction that caters to individuals' preferred learning styles—such as auditory or visual— improves educational outcomes. Although students may feel more engaged when teachers alter their instruction to meet their self-reported preferences, any potential benefits of teaching based on learning styles should not be overstated. Paula Tallal and colleagues tested this idea with a population of college-educated adults. Contrary to the expectations of learning style proponents, the researchers found no meaningful relationship between learning preference and learning outcomes based on the students' preferred mode of instruction. For example, students who considered themselves visual learners were no better at learning by reading than those who considered themselves auditory learners.

24. What is the primary purpose of the text?

(A) It presents a study by Paula Talal and colleagues to illustrate why caution is needed when making claims about the effects of instructional modes based on learning styles on learning outcomes.

(B) It highlights a study by Paula Talal and colleagues used to critique the methodology employed by earlier studies that found support for a certain hypothesis.

(C) It uses a study by Paula Talal and colleagues as an example of a flawed study that illustrates how knowledge about learning styles' effects is widely misunderstood.

(D) It describes how Paula Talal and colleagues sought to solve a problem related to how researchers understand the relationship between instruction tailored to learning styles and learning outcomes.

The excerpt below is from Barbara Jordan's 1975 Democratic Convention Keynote Address.

And now, what are those of us who are elected public officials supposed to do? We call ourselves "public servants" but I'll tell you this: We as public servants must set an example for the rest of the nation. It is hypocritical for the public official to admonish and exhort the people to uphold the common good if we are derelict in upholding the common good. More is required - - More is required of public officials than slogans and handshakes and press releases. More is required. We must hold ourselves strictly accountable. We must provide the people with a vision of the future.

25. What is the main purpose of the text?

(A) To absolve ordinary citizens of responsibility for uncivil behavior until politicians set a better example.

(B) To challenge public servants not to grow complacent with their own behavior.

(C) To enumerate specific ways public servants have caused societal woes by failing to fulfill their professional duties.

(D) To suggest that only those in elected office bear responsibility for upholding the public good.

Week 5: Vocabulary in Context

Pre-Lesson Reflection

Having a strong vocabulary is an important and often under-appreciated part of reading comprehension. Consider the sentence below that contains random words missing.

> The professor's _____ and _____ were _____ to his students: they _____ him as _____.

- **Reflect on how you felt reading through the sentence. How might this experience be comparable to reading a passage with unfamiliar words?**
- **Can you think of multiple ways the blanks can logically be filled?**
- **Depending on the words you choose, can the overall meaning of the sentence change? In what ways?**

You probably were able to come up with creative possibilities for the blanks. Without knowing the words, it is impossible to know what this sentence is saying, making it essentially incomprehensible.

Maybe the words in the blank are relatively positive words, as shown below.

*The professor's **charm** and **humor** were **endearing** to his students: they **regarded** him as **delightful**.*

Or maybe the words in the blank are more negative, as shown below.

*The professor's **unapproachability** and **condescension** were **frustrating** to his students: they **viewed** him as **unqualified**.*

Both these sentences have very different meanings. Although you do not need to know the literal meaning of every word you encounter in a passage, your ability to comprehend the passage will be seriously impaired if you do not understand the majority of the words in it. **Reading a passage without knowing what most of the words mean is just like reading a sentence with multiple blanks**. The more words you know, the better you will be at deducing what the unknown words mean. In the example above, for example, had you been told that the first blank was a word like "friendly," you could probably at the very least infer the second and last blanks would be words more positive tones.

While there is no set vocabulary list for the SAT, you should keep a running list of any words you come across in practice exams, study material (including in this book!), school, or outside reading that you do not know. You should not only look up these words' definitions, **but also see how they are used in sentences**, ideally **creating your own sentence**s so you can truly "own" the words. Luckily, most of the words tested on the vocabulary-in-context questions on the Digital SAT will be fairly common words that many students—even those without college level vocabulary— should know. The challenge on most questions is figuring out which word makes the most sense in the **context** of a specific sentence.

Consider the sentence below.

> Because Nora expected her project to take several weeks to complete, she was pleasantly _____ when she was able to finish it in only a few days by working efficiently.

What word do you think would make most sense in the blank**?**

We know Nora expected her project to take a long time to complete. In reality, she was able to complete it rather quickly. Thus, we can conclude that she felt **surprised.** "Surprised" would fit the blank nicely.

Let's look at one more example.

> Many employers have "clean desk" policies for their employees, believing that employees that have too many items on their desks will be distracted. But a study by Professors Craig Knight and Alexander Haslam shows that instead of hampering productivity, messy desks can actually _____ productivity, leading employees to generate more creative ideas.

"Instead of" signals that what the researchers discovered is opposite of "hampering," which means "hindering," or "slowing down." We also know that the employees generated more creative ideas. We can predict the word in the blank is a positive word that suggests productivity was increased. "Increase" or "boost" would be good predictions.

Vocabulary Fill-Ins

To answer vocabulary fill-in questions, do the following:
1) Read the entire passage.
2) Look for clues that hint at the meaning of the word in the blank.
3) Predict in your own words a word or phrase that fits the blank.
4) When possible, predict if the tone of the word or phrase in the blank is positive, negative, or neutral.
5) Examine the choices and see which matches your prediction.
6) If none matches your prediction, you can use the process of elimination to get rid of choices with the wrong tone or illogical meanings. You may need to read the sentence a few times to see how the word in the blank relates to other words in the passage.

Next, we will go over some of the common types of context clues. **But before we do, it is important to remember that not every question will neatly fall into one of these categories.** Thinking flexibly, using logic and common sense, and trusting your intuition are all important when approaching vocabulary-in-context questions.

Definition/Synonym/Description clues will either give you the literal definition of the word in the blank or include words with the same or very similar meanings (though perhaps in a different grammatical form). They may also provide a description of something so that its definition is implied. In the sentences below, the definition clues are underlined and the vocabulary words are in bold.
1) Benjy considers himself an **activist**: a person who campaigns for political and social change.
2) Lucia can be described as **diligent**: she is a hardworking student who is very conscientious in her studies.
3) Nneka made a beautiful mango lime cheesecake. Her **creation** was featured in a local magazine.
4) The ousted CEO argued that he was **misunderstood**: he claimed that his employees interpreted his constructive critiques of their workplace performance as personal attacks on their abilities.

In the first sentence we are given a literal definition of an activist.

In the second sentence, we are given synonyms for "diligent."

In the third sentence, "created" is a synonym for "made." The noun form of "created" ("creation") would make sense in context.

In the fourth sentence, we get a description of how the CEO felt he was misunderstood: he believed his employees misinterpreted (misunderstood) his critiques.

Contrast/Antonym clues include words that signal opposites or differences to the unknown word. Look out for transition words signaling contrasts (e.g., however, but, even though, although, though, while, conversely, on the other hand, instead, alternatively). The contrast clues are underlined for each bolded word.

1) While Sasha was frequently late to meetings in his personal life, at the office he was always **punctual.**
2) Rather than carefully reading the article, Joshua **skimmed** it.
3) Although the project was far from engaging, it was not as **tedious** as Clio expected.

The first sentence is a straightforward antonym clue. The opposite of "late" is "punctual." The transition word "while" signaled that a contrast was needed to show how Sasha is different in his personal life than at work.

In the second sentence, the transition "rather than" signals that we are looking for an opposite idea. Someone who does not carefully read something instead skims it.

The third sentence requires a bit more close reading. "Although" signals a contrast. Clio expected the project to be "far from engaging," or boring. We can predict Clio found the project *more engaging* than she expected, or *less tedious* (less boring) than she expected.

Cause and Effect clues will include a sentence that shows a cause and effect relationship (meaning one phenomenon causes another). Given a cause, infer an effect, and given an effect infer a cause. Look for transition words and phrases that signal such clues (e.g., cause, because, since, as a result, consequently, therefore, thus, so). In the examples below, the context clues are underlined for each bolded word.

1) Because the movie was so well-done, it earned critical **acclaim.**
2) As a result of customer **complaints** about unethical business practices, an investigation was launched into corruption at the large firm.
3) Dee argued that the city's problems had been worsened by outside advisors, so inviting them back would be **counterproductive.**

In the first example, as a result of the movie being well-done, it earned acclaim, or praise.

In the second case, an investigation resulted from complaints about the unethical practices.

In the third case, "so" signals a cause and effect relationship. Dee would likely think inviting the advisors back would be counterproductive if they worsened the city's problems (if they weren't helpful before, it makes no sense to invite them back).

Mini Activity 4: Using Context Clues

For each sentence, determine a logical word that fits each blank. Justify your answer by noting what type of clue you used or by explaining your reasoning.

Bodhi can be described as _____: he always finds quick and clever ways to overcome challenges.

1. What word might fit the blank?

2. Justify your answer.

Much is known about the friendship between the two philosophers because the number of letters they exchanged with one another was _____.

3. What word might fit the blank?

4. Justify your answer.

Impressionist artists _____ artistic traditions of their time, instead embracing abstract elements many art patrons found unappealing and unconventional.

5. What word might fit the blank?

6. Justify your answer.

While many companies _____ they like the idea of investing in solar panels in theory, they often are deterred from doing so in practice by high startup costs.

7. What word might fit the blank?

8. Justify your answer.

Since the author did not cite any data to back up his arguments that the environmental legislation was ineffective, many readers found his essay _____.

9. What word might fit the blank?

10. Justify your answer.

Although Inez is usually vocal during class debates, at the most recent debate she was uncharacteristically _____.

11. What word might fit the blank?

12. Justify your answer.

The persecution faced by abolitionists in the United States during the nineteenth century was not _____: reformers in past generations who challenged the status quo often faced similar pushback to their revolutionary ideas.

13. What word might fit the blank?

14. Justify your answer.

For the first sentence, we are given a definition clue describing Bodhi. Based on the description of him as someone who finds quick and clever solutions to challenges, you might predict that he is **resourceful** or **imaginative.**

The second sentence is a cause and effect clue. If much was known about the friendship, this suggests many letters were published between them. A logical prediction for the blank would be **abundant** or **plentiful.**

The third sentence presents a contrast clue. Instead of embracing artistic traditions, Impressionists embraced stylistic elements many people considered unconventional. Thus, we might predict the artists **rejected**, or **repudiated**, artistic traditions.

The fourth sentence presents a contrast clue, as indicated by "while." Many companies are deterred (discouraged) from investing in solar panels because of their high startup costs. The first part of the sentence should give a contrasting idea, namely one that shows they are open to investing in these panels. Possible words that fit the blank are **say** or **affirm.**

The fifth sentence presents a cause and effect clue. If the author did not use data to back up his arguments, we might conclude many people found his argument weak. Possible words that fit the blank are **unconvincing** or **unsupported.**

The sixth sentence is a contrast clue. While Inez is usually vocal during debates, at the last one she was uncharacteristically (atypically) the opposite of vocal. Possible words that fit the blank are **quiet** or **reserved.**

The seventh sentence includes the contrast word "not." Other reformers in past generations received similar pushback to abolitionists. We can conclude that the backlash abolitionists faced was typical, or NOT unusual. Possible words to fit the blank are **unusual** or **atypical.**

Sample 1

The global pet food market, which has shifted in focus from synthetic to natural products, generated nearly 100 billion US dollars in 2022, and some analysts, expecting to see continued growth, _____ the size of the market will increase by 4.4% each year through 2030.

Which choice best completes the text with the most logical and precise word or phrase?
    A) fret
    B) forecast
    C) refute
    D) preclude

We learn that the analysts are **expecting** to see continued growth. The word in the blank logically has the same meaning. We might predict that the word in the blank means something roughly along the lines of "predict" or "estimate." The tone of the word in the blank is likely neutral to positive, since experts expect the market to grow.

Choice A is too negative. While it could make sense to use the word "fret" when describing a prediction or expectation, this word would generally be reserved for negative situations ("fret"="worry").

Choice B is correct. "Forecast" means "predict" and makes sense in context.

Choice C does not make sense. Analysts expect the size of the market to grow. They don't refute (deny) this growth. C is also awkward and ungrammatical.

Choice D does not make sense logically. The analysts are not preventing or impeding the market size's increase, but instead they are predicting its increase in the future.

Sample 2

A 2021 discovery of apparent human footprints in New Mexico's White Sands National Park determined to be over 20,000 years old challenges conventional wisdom and may persuade the some archaeologists to _____ that the widely accepted theory that humans first arrived North America via the Bering Land Bridge only 13,500 years ago is incorrect.

Which choice best completes the text with the most logical and precise word or phrase?
  A) relinquish
  B) repudiate
  C) concede
  D) mandate

Because the discovery challenges conventional wisdom, it might persuade archeologists to admit, or acknowledge that the most widely accepted theory for how humans arrived in North America is wrong. The right answer should roughly mean "admit" or "accept."

Choice A is incorrect because "relinquish" means give up. This is the opposite of what we are looking for.

Choice B is similarly incorrect because "repudiate" means "reject." On the contrary, archaeologists might accept that the widely accepted theory is wrong.

Choice C is correct. "Concede" means to "admit" or "acknowledge." In light of evidence challenging the widely accepted theory, archaeologists might concede this theory is wrong.

Choice D is too extreme and is not precise. "Mandate" means "require" and does not make sense in context.

Vocabulary-in-Context

A smaller handful of vocabulary in context questions (likely about 1-2 per test) will ask you to determine the meaning of a particular word in a passage. Again, to answer these questions, use the context of the entire sentence or the sentences surrounding it to determine its meaning. **When the correct answer choice is substituted for the original word in the passage, the sentence should make sense. Thus, you should "plug in" the correct answer choice in place of the original word in the passage.**
Note that more than one choice will probably be *a correct meaning* of the word in some context.

Consider the following sentences.
1) **Cause and Effect Clue:** The judge has a reputation for making **fair** rulings. He is thus regarded as a beacon of justice.

In this case, fair means "just" or "equitable." We are given the effect of his rulings (he is seen as a beacon, or model, of justice), and the word "fair" is the cause for why he is viewed that way.

2) **Definition/Synonym Clue:** It will take a **fair** amount of time to complete the essay: it requires *considerable* thought and planning.

In this case fair means "considerable," or "moderately large." It will take an appreciable amount of time to plan the essay before writing it.

3) **Contrast Clue:** His project was **fair**, but it was not exceptional enough to qualify him for a raise.

In this case "fair" means "adequate" or "**not** excellent or poor." The project was not excellent enough to earn him a raise.

Tip: Usually, the most obvious or common meaning of a term is listed as an incorrect answer choice. For example, on a multiple choice question, the word "hammer" is more likely to mean "to form" or "construct" (as in "hammer out an agreement") than to literally mean "beat" (as in "hammer nails into a board").

To answer vocabulary-in-context questions, do the following:
1) Read the entire passage.
2) Look for clues that hint at the meaning of the tested word.
3) Predict in your own words a word or phrase can replace the tested word.
4) When possible, predict if the tone of the word or phrase in the blank is positive, negative, or neutral.
5) Examine the choices and see which matches your prediction.
6) If none matches your prediction, use the process of elimination to get rid of choices with the wrong tone or illogical meanings. You may need to read the sentence a few times to see how the word in the blank relates to other words in the passage.

Sample 3

The excerpt below is from *Life of Pi* by Yan Martell.

If we, citizens, do not <u>support</u> our artists, then we sacrifice our imagination on the altar of crude reality and we end up believing in nothing and having worthless dreams.

As used in the text, "support" most nearly means
(A) authenticate
(B) ratify
(C) champion
(D) brace

The sentence gives a consequence of not supporting artists, namely sacrificing imagination. Although "support" is a word with many meanings, we can predict it likely means "back," "encourage," or "defend." The public must provide backing to artists so that they continue making art.

Choice A does not make sense. To authenticate something means to validate that it is genuine (an archaeologist might authenticate that an artifact claimed to be from ancient Rome is not a fake).

Choice B does not make sense. "Ratify" means to give formal consent to or make legally valid (as when a government ratifies a treaty).

Choice C is correct. When you champion a group of people, you advocate for them, back them up, or stand up for them. Citizens have a responsibility to show support for artists.

Choice D is incorrect. "Brace" means to provide physical support that helps steady or strengthen something (as when columns are used to brace a part of a building).

Sample 4

The excerpt below is from Barbara Jordan's 1976 Democratic Convention Keynote Address.

We are a people in a <u>quandary</u> about the present. We are a people in search of our future. We are a people in search of a national community. We are a people trying not only to solve the problems of the present, unemployment, inflation, but we are attempting on a larger scale to fulfill the promise of America. We are attempting to fulfill our national purpose, to create and sustain a society in which all of us are equal.

As used in the text, the word "quandary" most nearly means
(A) predicament
(B) transition
(C) blockage
(D) revelation

In context, we learn that the people are conflicted and confused about where to go next: how to form a national community, solve their problems, and fulfill their purpose. We might predict that quandary means "dilemma."

Choice A is correct. A predicament is a dilemma, or a situation that poses a conflict.

Choice B is incorrect. While the country might be in a period of transition (change), "transition about the present" is not a logical phrase. Nor is it negative enough in tone.

Choice C is not precise. It does not make sense to say people are in a blockage (obstruction) "about" a time period.

Choice D is not precise. A revelation (realization) would not make sense in context. If anything one could say "we had a revelation (realization) that we are in a quandary (predicament)."

Drill 5

Túpac Amaru II. was one of the most _____ historical figures in Peru during Spanish civil rule. Among his notable actions were using his position in the Spanish government to promote Indigenous rights and leading a large rebellion against the colonial government. While his rebellion failed, it inspired native populations in Peru, leading to wars that eventually established Peruvian independence.

1. Which choice best completes the text with the most logical and precise word or phrase?
(A) significant
(B) typical
(C) reserved
(D) irritable

Planetary scientist Sara Mazrouei notes that physical evidence on the Earth might not accurately _____ the history of celestial objects like asteroids that have struck its surface. This is because a variety of factors—such as rainfall, plate tectonics, and weathering—remove many craters indicative of past impacts.

2. Which choice best completes the text with the most logical and precise word or phrase?
   (A) reflect
   (B) refract
   (C) contend
   (D) extend

Perovskite solar cells have the potential to replace silicon, thus lowering the cost of solar electricity; however, their inability to withstand inclement weather and diverse temperature conditions without corroding has been a roadblock to their use. But a team of researchers may have found a way to _____ this obstacle: by treating perovskite solar cells with 1,3-bis(diphenylphosphino) propane (DPPP), the researchers showed it is possible to increase these cells' durability after continuous operation in outdoor conditions.

3. Which choice best completes the text with the most logical and precise word or phrase?
   (A) neglect
   (B) demonstrate
   (C) overcome
   (D) theorize

Psychological experts note that while some actions, like frequent absenteeism, are often obvious signs of employee burnout, employers should be aware of less _____ signs of job burnout in their employees and offer them support to better thrive in their jobs.

4. Which choice best completes the text with the most logical and precise word or phrase?
   (A) subtle
   (B) recognizable
   (C) quirky
   (D) commonplace

In 2022, while on a mission to obtain samples from Mars's landscape, the Perseverance (a robotic motor vehicle), encountered an unexpected challenge that temporarily halted its progress: debris in the form of rocks. Scientists from Earth were able to address the problem once they determined the cause, and the sample _____ process continued.

5. Which choice best completes the text with the most logical and precise word or phrase?
   (A) depiction
   (B) collection
   (C) rejection
   (D) interrogation

Scientists working in the nanotechnology field spend much of their time _____ ultra-small substances: they examine matter at the atomic and molecular scale with hopes of applying the knowledge gained for industrial purposes. For example, nanosensors in food packaging can be used to detect food contaminants.

6. Which choice best completes the text with the most logical and precise word or phrase?
   (A) portraying
   (B) producing
   (C) inspecting
   (D) determining

If a poinsettia plant, also known as a Christmas flower, has yellowish leaves and lacks intact bracts, it likely has suffered insufficient light, over-watering, or a lack of nitrogen; by contrast, _____ poinsettias should have deep green leaves and brilliant red bracts.

7. Which choice best completes the text with the most logical and precise word or phrase?
   (A) unsightly
   (B) healthy
   (C) gaunt
   (D) rare

Major League Soccer (MLS) player and children's literacy advocate Kevin Hartman's _____ for his two passions culminated in him authoring *Boots Saves the Day*, a story about soccer produced specifically for children.

8. Which choice best completes the text with the most logical and precise word or phrase?
   (A) distaste
   (B) effusion
   (C) excitement
   (D) nonchalance

When scholars at the University of Germany argued that the Shigir Idol—the oldest known piece of ritual art in the world—was 900 years older than previously believed, many scientists readily _____ this conclusion: the team's scientific analysis told such a convincing tale that the artifact was produced around 12,500 years ago.

9. Which choice best completes the text with the most logical and precise word or phrase?
   (A) debunked
   (B) believed
   (C) refuted
   (D) downplayed

In the United States, Congress has the power to create laws regulating activities that impact the environment, including actions that pollute air. However, Congress can authorize independent agencies of the federal government, such as the Environmental Protection Agency, to _____ such laws by through the creation of technical regulations in accordance with the laws Congresses passes.

10. Which choice best completes the text with the most logical and precise word or phrase?

    (A) contemplate

    (B) emulate

    (C) suppose

    (D) implement

A fundamental method of communication based on a system of dots and dashes that does not require specialized machines, Morse Code enjoys _____ use in the twenty-first century thanks to its versatility: it remains highly popular in a variety of professional settings, such as the Navy, Coast Guard, aviation industry, and aeronautical fields.

11. Which choice best completes the text with the most logical and precise word or phrase?

    (A) obsolete

    (B) cautious

    (C) widespread

    (D) conscripted

The University of Oxford announced that it would credit Christopher Marlowe as co-author of three of Shakespeare's *Henry VI* plays. Though this decision was based on careful textual analysis revealing signature aspects of Marlowe's vocabulary and writing style, other scholars do not think evidence of Marlowe's influence on these plays means that the plays resulted from direct _____ between the playwrights.

12. Which choice best completes the text with the most logical and precise word or phrase?

    (A) collaboration

    (B) osmosis

    (C) mediation

    (D) categorization

The termination of some high speed rail projects in the United States challenged a journalist's assertion that high speed rail would gain significant traction in the United States. However, these setbacks do not _____ the journalist's projection entirely, as some private companies are actively working on high speed rail projects, though, at the very least, the timeline for the journalist's prediction becoming a reality will be delayed.

13. Which choice best completes the text with the most logical and precise word or phrase?

    (A) concur

    (B) invalidate

    (C) clash

    (D) protest

While the influence of ideals from the European Enlightenment on the United States Constitution should not be regarded as _____—for example, the founders drew on the works of English philosopher John Locke as an inspiration for the structure of government laid out in the Constitution—some scholars argue that the Iroquois nation actually had a stronger influence on the Constitution's development.

14. Which choice best completes the text with the most logical and precise word or phrase?

(A) paramount
(B) unimportant
(C) providential
(D) beneficial

For his 2018 exhibition *Domestic Space*, B. Wurtz produced sculptors that were lauded for being _____: he refashioned traditional household objects by stripping them of their traditional roles, revealing their aesthetic potential. For example, he repurposes a lampshade to resemble a rocket about to set off into interstellar space.

15. Which choice best completes the text with the most logical and precise word or phrase?

(A) subdued
(B) ineffable
(C) baffling
(D) inventive

For many years, glial cells were considered mere support cells for neurons, but research suggests they are more _____ than previously thought; beyond providing protection and nutrition for neurons, glial cells have been implicated in key neural developmental mechanisms, such as regulating neurotransmitter release and assisting in synaptic transmission, among other roles.

16. Which choice best completes the text with the most logical and precise word or phrase?

(A) ancillary
(B) obscure
(C) versatile
(D) homogeneous

In many industries, managing workflow operations across diverse platforms leads to _____, wasting time and resources. Mechanisms that enhance transparency, such as using a single platform to keep a single system of records across departments, can help companies work more effectively.

17. Which choice best completes the text with the most logical and precise word or phrase?

(A) expediency
(B) inefficiency
(C) altercations
(D) alacrity

The concept of the "iron triangle" highlights the _____ web of alliances that can exist between special interest groups, legislators, and bureaucrats: special interest groups help fund the campaigns of legislators who promise to create laws that benefit the interest groups; the legislators provide funding and support for bureaucrats, who in turn implement legislation; and special interest groups provide bureaucrats with industry information in exchange for favorable regulations and contracts.

    18. Which choice best completes the text with the most logical and precise word or phrase?

        (A) intricate

        (B) aboveboard

        (C) arcane

        (D) unintelligible

Many experts note that although there are currently great concerns about the amount of misinformation in digital spaces, steps will be taken to address the issues this problem causes. While some experts _____ that efforts to combat misinformation will come from educational interventions that teach digital literacy and civic innovations that protect information quality, others speculate that more sophisticated fact-checking technology will be of utmost importance.

    19. Which choice best completes the text with the most logical and precise word or phrase?

        (A) establish

        (B) hypothesize

        (C) prove

        (D) recant

The Industrial Revolution of the late eighteenth to early nineteenth century saw one of the most rapid and significant transitions in manufacturing processes in continental Europe and the United States, with machine production largely replacing hand production in a variety of industries. Some scholars argue that a small number of innovations, such as advancements of steam power and iron production, acted as catalysts that led to _____ changes in the way many products were produced.

    20. Which choice best completes the text with the most logical and precise word or phrase?

        (A) abrupt

        (B) impending

        (C) ruinous

        (D) evasive

Due to their abstract nature, use of surprising juxtapositions, and inclusion of elements of disorder, paintings from the Surrealist Movement often have meanings that are difficult to _____ and are therefore subject to scholarly debate among art experts.

    21. Which choice best completes the text with the most logical and precise word or phrase?

        (A) decipher

        (B) relegate

        (C) concede

        (D) fete

Gertrude Stein's abstract writing style—which often involves violations of traditional grammar rules— is sometimes panned by critics for being unreadable to the average person. Other scholars argue that Stein's refusal to adhere to traditional linguistic rules freed her to create her own meanings and dismantle preconceived notions of reality. Thus, Stein's unconventional writing style does not indicate that she was a _____ creator of unintelligible gibberish; rather, she made intentional syntactical choices that showcased her intellectual merit.

22. Which choice best completes the text with the most logical and precise word or phrase?

    (A) provocative

    (B) learned

    (C) brilliant

    (D) careless

Marian Y.L. Wong and others at the University of Wollongong are studying a species of coral-dwelling goby from the genus *Paragobiodon* to determine whether resource limitation has _____ effect on reproductive success— that is, to see if variations in the availability of resources such as food are associated with variations in the number of eggs hatched between different members of the same species.

23. Which choice best completes the text with the most logical and precise word or phrase?

    (A) a considerable

    (B) an indistinguishable

    (C) an elusive

    (D) an adequate

An architectural firm in Toronto was hired to make an Indigenous library that incorporated traditional Indigenous building materials, sustainable building practices, and designs, but it did not merely _____ traditions; it incorporated twenty-first century amenities, such as mechanical heating and cooling systems.

24. Which choice best completes the text with the most logical and precise word or phrase?

    (A) correlate with

    (B) adhere to

    (C) improve on

    (D) contend with

Some adherents to traditional economic models have _____ that humans are rational economic actors: that is, they seek to pay as little as possible and maximize their self-interest. The field of behavioral economics, however, challenges this supposition based on data that humans do not always behave logically when making purchasing decisions.

25. Which choice best completes the text with the most logical and precise word or phrase?

    (A) lamented

    (B) questioned

    (C) surmised

    (D) denied

Some educational professionals believe that one goal of education should be to expose and nurture _____ talents present in children. For example, students who show emerging signs of interest or aptitude in music should be given the chance to develop their musical skills, such as through formal lessons and opportunities to perform in ensembles.

26. Which choice best completes the text with the most logical and precise word or phrase?
    (A) acclaimed
    (B) ineffable
    (C) predestined
    (D) latent

For David Adjaye, being _____ is integral to his architectural design process. For each of his projects, he carefully studies research about the location of the building, including its local governing structure, history and culture of its people, and geologic attributes. As a result, each building has a unique aesthetic that tells the story of the people for whom it is built.

27. Which choice best completes the text with the most logical and precise word or phrase?
    (A) observant
    (B) informed
    (C) spontaneous
    (D) collaborative

According to some economic experts, compensation and benefits are often _____ other factors when employees evaluate their job satisfaction. For example, a study found that salary has a relatively small influence on employees' self-reported job satisfaction while company culture, quality of senior leadership, and career opportunities within an organization were important influences.

28. Which choice best completes the text with the most logical and precise word or phrase?
    (A) consistent with
    (B) immaterial to
    (C) contingent on
    (D) eclipsed by

Artist Paul Kremer used traditional artistic tools such as paintbrushes and canvases to _____ an original series of paintings titled "Blooms," but he leveraged artificial intelligence (AI) technology to manipulate his paintings; he relies on this technology to improve his coding skills, import new color palettes, and produce new ideas.

29. Which choice best completes the text with the most logical and precise word or phrase?
    (A) generate
    (B) authenticate
    (C) restore
    (D) emulate

Unlike many monarchs in the Middle Ages, who needed to do little to justify their right to rule, Henry IV, plagued by a legitimacy crisis, needed extensive documentation and was forced to fight a civil war to _____ his claim to the throne.

30. Which choice best completes the text with the most logical and precise word or phrase?

(A) renege

(B) concede

(C) buttress

(D) annotate

In addition to being an accomplished author herself, Toni Morrison was _____ opening up opportunities for other Black writers, using her position at the publishing company Random House to publish and edit the works of Black writers, gaining them publicity.

31. Which choice best completes the text with the most logical and precise word or phrase?

(A) an advocate of

(B) an addition to

(C) a beneficiary of

(D) a confounder with

A brain stimulation technique known as transcranial magnetic stimulation (TMS) generally alters reaction time profiles, but it can also produce_____ responses in subjects; such responses can include automatic movements such as blinking or jaw clamping.

32. Which choice best completes the text with the most logical and precise word or phrase?

(A) mandatory

(B) intentional

(C) strenuous

(D) involuntary

A 2011 study co-authored by David Bennett found evidence of 10 free-floating planets with roughly the mass of Jupiter, a much greater number than Bennett's team expected to find based on known mechanisms for how planets become wanderers. A later study challenged this finding, suggesting that many Jupiter-sized stars were _____ classified as Jupiter-sized planets instead.

33. Which choice best completes the text with the most logical and precise word or phrase?

(A) notably

(B) robustly

(C) inaccurately

(D) presciently

Jaune Quick-to-See Smith is not only a talented artist but also a celebrated activist who has worked diligently to educate the general American public about American Indian culture; her persistent efforts to foster respect for Indigenous cultures included _____ lecturing about Indigenous issues in universities, museums, and other public cultural settings.

34. Which choice best completes the text with the most logical and precise word or phrase?
    (A) unrehearsed
    (B) regular
    (C) homogeneous
    (D) spontaneous

Given that climate change is a complex phenomenon that raises political, ecological, economic, health, and quality of life issues, among others, the solutions for how to address it in a systematic way that protects human life and minimizes societal disruption are not _____.

35. Which choice best completes the text with the most logical and precise word or phrase?
    (A) straightforward
    (B) nuanced
    (C) rigorous
    (D) learnable

Some people assert that business practices that improve a business's bottom line (profit) and those that are ecologically friendly are rarely _____ in a world where measures taken to maximize profits have a secondary effect of polluting or damaging the environment. Yet a 2014 study by the University of Arkansas challenged this idea and showed that businesses engaging in environmentally friendly practices often stand to both directly and indirectly benefit economically, such as through reduced costs, increased revenues, and increased appeal to prospective employees.

36. Which choice best completes the text with the most logical and precise word or phrase?
    (A) compatible
    (B) deviatory
    (C) agreeable
    (D) incongruous

Citizen science, a situation in which volunteers collaborate with scientists to expand scientific knowledge, is deeply rooted in United States history, as such partnerships have proven invaluable in accelerating the pace of scientific research. The Sloan Digital Sky Survey (SDSS) is one prominent _____ of the citizen science model: participants can submit data to help scientists at Oxford University classify galaxies as spiral or elliptical. As a result of contributions by ordinary citizens, researchers deepened their understanding of how galaxies form and evolve.

37. Which choice best completes the text with the most logical and precise word or phrase?
    (A) illustration
    (B) anomaly
    (C) rebuttal
    (D) forgery

Many bacteria use nitrogen gas to produce ammonia, a compound that is useful to plants, but low nitrogen content in soil can limit plants' growth. Legumes, whose leaves contain large amounts of nitrogen gas, have _____ the problem of low nitrogen supply in nitrogen-depleted soils by entering into a symbiotic relationship with bacteria from the *Rhizobium* genus: the plant supplies food and shelter in exchange for ammonia.

38. Which choice best completes the text with the most logical and precise word or phrase?

(A) intimated

(B) solved

(C) clarified

(D) synchronized

Jazz pianist Dave Brubeck declined to _____ the conventions of the genre in which he played, and he was notable for thwarting expectations about what audiences wanted to hear by experimenting with unusual time signatures and tonalities.

39. Which choice best completes the text with the most logical and precise word or phrase?

(A) become familiar with

(B) disavow

(C) conform to

(D) question

It may seem that common "street food" and upscale fine dining can rarely _____, each belonging in its own sphere. But chefs like Jorge Vallejo challenge this idea, claiming the distinction between "high cuisine" and "popular cuisine" is grounded in prejudice rather than in reality: in his own fine dining restaurant in Mexico City, Vallejo draws on inspiration from the street food scene, elevating popular foods such as tacos into elegant displays that highlight their versatility.

40. Which choice best completes the text with the most logical and precise word or phrase?

(A) diverge

(B) intersect

(C) withstand

(D) digress

The main character of Pearl Buck's *The Good Earth,* Wang Lung, is a hardworking farmer in the village of Anhui; a vocation which is not _____ in Buck's novels: many of her works richly portray the lives of peasant characters.

41. Which choice best completes the text with the most logical and precise word or phrase?

(A) representative

(B) infallible

(C) unprofitable

(D) atypical

One of the hallmarks of most successful fictional films is a compelling script, but Gaspar Noé _____ this tradition: this rejection of convention is apparent in his film *Climax*, in which actors worked off a short outline and improvised extensively, a daring move that led to generally positive reception from critics.

42. Which choice best completes the text with the most logical and precise word or phrase?
   - (A) recanted
   - (B) deliberated
   - (C) repudiated
   - (D) honored

A team of graduate students led by Eugenia Gold used computerized tomography to investigate the skull of *Raphus cucullatus*, the dodo bird. The team found that its brain to body ratio was _____ those of animals with strong navigation skills, like modern-day pigeons, suggesting the dodo might also possess impressive cognitive capacities.

43. Which choice best completes the text with the most logical and precise word or phrase?
   - (A) anathema to
   - (B) comparable to
   - (C) independent of
   - (D) exceeded by

In *Democratic Deficit: Critical Citizens Revisited*, Pippa Norris discusses the concept of a "democratic deficit," which is reflected in the gap between many people's approval of democratic ideals and their dissatisfaction with the actual performance of democratic states. Such _____ attitudes about democracy sometimes culminate in citizens electing leaders who openly flout democratic norms.

44. Which choice best completes the text with the most logical and precise word or phrase?
   - (A) zealous
   - (B) ambivalent
   - (C) malevolent
   - (D) byzantine

In the United States' two party system of government, minor party candidates are rarely able to compete in a way that will allow them to gain a substantial number of seats in the federal government. Still, some scholars argue that such parties serve important functions, such as providing a valve for voters to express their discontent at the two major parties, forcing the major parties to adapt in order to win over minor party voters in future elections: to some voters, minor party candidates provide them with _____ alternative that allows them to stay engaged in the political process and make their voices heard.

45. Which choice best completes the text with the most logical and precise word or phrase?
   - (A) a disconcerting
   - (B) an immutable
   - (C) a palatable
   - (D) a fiery

Ingestion of plastics poses a serious threat to the health of many birds, who often mistake such plastics for food. Because the birds most vulnerable to consuming plastics are often the least charismatic species and are the most difficult birds to track, more vigilant monitoring of such species is _____ in order to protect them.

46. Which choice best completes the text with the most logical and precise word or phrase?
   (A) superfluous
   (B) warranted
   (C) histrionic
   (D) alarming

Freud argued that tendentious humor, which requires a victim as the object of its joke, is superior at provoking amusement than non-tendentious humor that relies more on innocent wordplay. However, to make tendentious humor less offensive to audiences, he argued that both types of humor should be combined: people are more likely to find tendentious humor socially acceptable when couched in language that is more superficially _____ yet biting under the surface.

47. Which choice best completes the text with the most logical and precise word or phrase?
   (A) melodramatic
   (B) innocuous
   (C) daft
   (D) evasive

Economic theories have explained differences in the economic performance between central locations, such as large urban centers, and small remote locations. Because most economic activity clusters centrally, Professors Caroline Buts and Phedon Nicolaides argue that _____ islands are often at a competitive disadvantage: due to their physical isolation, low connectivity to the mainland, and small economies of scale, investment decisions by governments often favor the mainland.

48. Which choice best completes the text with the most logical and precise word or phrase?
   (A) peripheral
   (B) clandestine
   (C) nuanced
   (D) elusive

The art of Ludovico Caracci drew on many _____ influences that blended classical and Renaissance traditions: line from Michelangelo; chiaroscuro—strong contrasts between light and dark—from Antonio da Correggio; and emphasis on symmetry and grace from Raphael.

49. Which choice best completes the text with the most logical and precise word or phrase?
   (A) disparate
   (B) interchangeable
   (C) acrimonious
   (D) perpendicular

While there have been many studies on the psychological phenomenon known as the testing effect—the idea that people learn better from being quizzed on learned content than from simply rereading it—there had long been a _____ of studies that examined the testing effect in the context of authentic educational materials. This motivated Cynthia Wooldridge and colleagues to examine the effectiveness of the testing effect in a classroom setting when quiz questions were both similar to and identical to final exam questions.

50. Which choice best completes the text with the most logical and precise word or phrase?

(A) preponderance

(B) quagmire

(C) dearth

(D) plausibility

In Jane Austen's *Pride and Prejudice,* the protagonist defies _____ social traditions about marriage, instead choosing to marry for love rather than social standing. Still, she does end up marrying a character within her social class, thus conforming to societal expectations.

51. Which choice best completes the text with the most logical and precise word or phrase?

(A) nuanced

(B) progressive

(C) compulsory

(D) prescribed

In Sherry Ortner's *New Jersey Dreaming*, she took a new approach to ethnographic writing, rejecting the idea that culture was _____ force that is shared by a group of people living in a common physical location. Rather, she argued that culture is constantly changing and permeates beyond geographic boundaries.

52. Which choice best completes the text with the most logical and precise word or phrase?

(A) an idiosyncratic

(B) a static

(C) a liminal

(D) a dynamic

The empirical evidence in support of the ecologist's contention about the positive relationship between island size and abundance of predatory spiders is _____ at best. To be more convincing, it would need to explain why smaller islands in the Baja California ecosystem actually often have higher abundances of such predators than larger islands have.

53. Which choice best completes the text with the most logical and precise word or phrase?

(A) cogent

(B) provocative

(C) tenuous

(D) insipid

The excerpt below is from Albert Lutuli's Nobel Prize acceptance speech.

It is so easy sometimes to hide under groups when you do very little for a cause. Here the stress is on the individual, so making peace, no less than war, is the concern of every man and woman on earth, whether they be in Senegal or Berlin, in Washington or in the shattered towns of South Africa. However <u>humble</u> the place, it can make its contribution also, it is expected to make its contribution to peace.

54. As used in the text, "humble" most nearly means
    (A) self-effacing.
    (B) undeserving.
    (C) degrading.
    (D) unremarkable.

The excerpt below is from *Song of Solomon* by Toni Morrison, and it describes the character of Hagar's reflections on the character of Milkman.

In fact her maturity and blood kinship converted her passion to fever, so it was more affliction than affection. It literally knocked her down at night, and raised her up in the morning, for when she dragged herself off to bed, having spent another day without his presence, her heart beat like a gloved fist against her ribs. And in the morning, long before she was fully awake, she felt a <u>longing</u> so bitter and tight it yanked her out of a sleep swept clean of dreams.

55. As used in the text, "longing" most nearly means
    (A) yearning.
    (B) extending.
    (C) flavor.
    (D) repulsion.

The excerpt below is from "The Progress of 50 Years" by Lucy Stone.

Half a century ago women were at an infinite disadvantage in regard to their occupations. The idea that their <u>sphere</u> was at home, and only at home, was like a band of steel on society. But the spinning-wheel and the loom, which had given employment to women, had been superseded by machinery, and something else had to take their places.

56. As used in the text, "sphere" most nearly means
    (A) domain.
    (B) orb.
    (C) department.
    (D) pastime.

The excerpt below is from Douglas MacArthur's "Duty, Honor, and Country" speech.

Coming from a profession I have served so long, and a people I have loved so well, it fills me with an emotion I cannot <u>express.</u> But this award is not intended primarily to honor a personality, but to symbolize a great moral code -- the code of conduct and chivalry of those who guard this beloved land of culture and ancient descent.

  57. As used in the text, "express" most nearly means

   (A) put into words.
   (B) represent symbolically.
   (C) send quickly.
   (D) force out by squeezing.

The excerpt below is adapted from the National Institute of Health's article, "Scientists Plug into a Learning a Brain."

After determining the intrinsic manifold, the team reprogrammed the map between neural activity and cursor movement. For instance, if a firing pattern originally caused the cursor to move to the top of the screen, then the interface would move the cursor to the bottom. The team then observed whether the animals could learn to <u>generate</u> the appropriate neural activity patterns to compensate for the changes.

  58. As used in the text, "generate" most nearly means

   (A) breed.
   (B) prevent.
   (C) produce.
   (D) define.

The excerpt below is from Lucretia Mott's speech "Discourse on Women."

Why should not woman seek to be a reformer? If she is to fear to exercise her <u>reason,</u> and her noblest powers, lest she should be thought to "attempt to act the man," and not "acknowledge his supremacy;" if she is to be satisfied with the narrow sphere assigned her by man, nor aspire to a higher, lest she should transcend the bounds of female delicacy; truly it is a mournful prospect for woman.

  59. As used in the text, the word "reason" most nearly means

   (A) natural instincts.
   (B) intellectual capacities.
   (C) justified excuses.
   (D) subtle pretexts.

The excerpt below is from Eleanor Roosevelt's speech "Adopting the Declaration of Human Rights."

Basic human rights are simple and easily understood: freedom of speech and a free press; freedom of religion and worship; freedom of assembly and the right of petition; the right of men to be secure in their homes and free from unreasonable search and seizure and from arbitrary arrest and punishment.

60. As used in the text, "basic" most nearly means

(A) easy.
(B) introductory.
(C) fundamental.
(D) undeveloped.

The excerpt below is from "[Like a White Stone]" by Anna Akhmatova.

The ancient gods changed men to things, but left them
A consciousness that smoldered endlessly,
That splendid sorrows might endure forever.
And you are changed into a memory.

61. As used in the text, "endure" most nearly means

(A) tolerate.
(B) last.
(C) transform.
(D) undergo.

The excerpt below is from Barbara Jordan's 1976 Democratic Convention (DNC) Keynote Address.

I, Barbara Jordan, am a keynote speaker. When -- A lot of years passed since 1832, and during that time it would have been most unusual for any national political party to ask Barbara Jordan to deliver a keynote address. But tonight, here I am. And I feel -- I feel that notwithstanding the past that my presence here is one additional bit of evidence that the American Dream need not forever be deferred.

62. As used in the text, "deferred" most nearly means

(A) referred.
(B) exempted.
(C) respected.
(D) postponed.

The excerpt below is from *The Importance of Being Earnest* by Oscar Wilde.

GWENDOLEN.
Oh! It is strange he never mentioned to me that he had a ward. How secretive of him! He grows more interesting hourly. I am not sure, however, that the news inspires me with feelings of unmixed delight. [Rising and going to her.] I am very fond of you, Cecily; I have liked you ever since I met you! But I am <u>bound</u> to state that now that I know that you are Mr. Worthing's ward, I cannot help expressing a wish you were—well, just a little older than you seem to be—and not quite so very alluring in appearance. In fact, if I may speak candidly—

CECILY.
Pray do! I think that whenever one has anything unpleasant to say, one should always be quite candid.

63. As used in the text, "bound" most nearly means
(A) attached.
(B) destined.
(C) obliged.
(D) reluctant.

The following passage is adapted from the National Institute of Health's article "Researchers investigate how a Developing Brain is Assembled."

Although scientists have identified a number of important proteins that determine how neurons navigate during brain formation, it's largely unknown how all of these proteins interact in a living organism. Model animals, despite their differences from humans, have already revealed much about human physiology because they are much simpler and easier to understand. In this case, researchers chose Caenorhabditis elegans (C. elegans), because it has only 302 neurons, 222 of which form while the worm is still an embryo. While some of these neurons go to the worm nerve ring (brain) they also spread along the ventral nerve cord, which is broadly <u>analogous to</u> the spinal cord in humans.

64. As used in the text, "analogous to" most nearly means
(A) identical to.
(B) separate from.
(C) comparable to.
(D) resultant of.

The excerpt below is from E.M. Foster's *A Room With A View*. Lucy is vacationing in Italy with her cousin Charlotte. They are upset with the rooms they have been placed in at their hotel.

She hastened after her cousin, who had already disappeared through the curtains—curtains which smote one in the face, and seemed heavy with more than cloth. Beyond them stood the unreliable Signora, bowing good-evening to her guests, and supported by 'Enery, her little boy, and Victorier, her daughter. It made a <u>curious</u> little scene, this attempt of the Cockney to convey the grace and geniality of the South. And even more curious was the drawing-room, which attempted to rival the solid comfort of a Bloomsbury boarding-house. Was this really Italy?

65. As used in the text, "curious" most nearly means

(A) inquisitive.

(B) peculiar.

(C) modest.

(D) unkempt.

The excerpt below is adapted from *The Picture of Dorian Gray* by Oscar Wilde. The excerpt below describes Dorian.

He would examine with <u>minute</u> care, and often with a monstrous and terrible delight, the hideous lines that seared the wrinkling forehead or crawled around the heavy sensual mouth, wondering sometimes which were the more horrible, the signs of sin or the signs of age. He would place his white hands beside the coarse bloated hands of the picture, and smile. He mocked the misshapen body and the failing limbs.

66. As used in the text, "minute" most nearly means

(A) meticulous.
(B) timely.
(C) microscopic.
(D) insignificant.

The quote below is from *The Merchant of Venice* by William Shakespeare

The <u>quality</u> of mercy is not strained.
It droppeth as the gentle rain from heaven
Upon the place beneath. It is twice blessed:

67. As used in the text, "quality" most nearly means

(A) attribute.
(B) eminence.
(C) criterion.
(D) achievement.

Below is Robert La Follette's 1917 speech, "Senate Address on Free Speech in War Time Title." In context, he is discussing the right of citizens to criticize World War I.

And, sir, this is the ground on which I stand. I <u>maintain</u> that Congress has the right and the duty to declare the objects of the war and the people have the right and the obligation to discuss it.

American citizens may hold all shades of opinion as to the war; one citizen may glory in it another may deplore it, each has the same right to voice his judgment. An American citizen may think and say that we are not justified in prosecuting this war for the purpose of dictating the form of government which shall be maintained by our enemy or our ally, and not be subject to punishment at law.

68. As used in the text, "maintain" most nearly means
    (A) keep.
    (B) affirm.
    (C) continue.
    (D) sustain.

The excerpt below is adapted from Theodore Roosevelt's 1906 speech "The Man with the Muckraker." Roosevelt is discussing "muckrakers," journalists who exposed corruption in business and government.

An epidemic of <u>indiscriminate</u> assault upon character does no good, but very great harm. The soul of every scoundrel is gladdened whenever an honest man is assailed, or even when a scoundrel is untruthfully assailed.

69. As used in the text, "indiscriminate" most nearly means
    (A) systematic.
    (B) undiscerning.
    (C) homogeneous.
    (D) candid.

The poem below is "The Serving Girl" by Gladys May Casely Hayford.

The calabash wherein she served my food,
Was smooth and polished as sandalwood:
Fish, as white as the foam of the sea,
Peppered, and golden fried for me.
She brought palm wine that carelessly slips
From the sleeping palm tree's honeyed lips.
But who can guess, or even <u>surmise</u>
The countless things she served with her eyes?

70. As used in the text, "surmise" most nearly means
    (A) infer.
    (B) command.
    (C) puzzle.
    (D) praise.

The excerpt below is from Frederick Douglass's speech "What to the Slave is Fourth of July?"

There is hope in the thought, and hope is much needed, under the dark clouds which lower above the horizon. The eye of the reformer is met with angry flashes, portending disastrous times; but his heart may well beat lighter at the thought that America is young, and that she is still in the <u>impressible</u> stage of her existence.

71. As used in the text, "impressible" most nearly means
    (A) rigid.
    (B) impressive.
    (C) eminent.
    (D) pliable.

The poem below is "South Street" by Edward Silvera.

South Street is not beautiful,
But the songs of people there
Hold the beauty of the jungle,
And the fervidness of prayer.

South Street has no mansions,
But the hands of South Street men
Built pyramids along the Nile
That Time has failed to <u>rend</u>.

72. As used in the text, "rend" most nearly means
    (A) construct.
    (B) perceive.
    (C) destroy.
    (D) heal.

Sometimes you will be given two passages related to the same topic. Typically, the passages will be related to each other in one of the following ways.
1) They will take opposite positions on the same issue.
   - Example: Text 1 argues that the causes of the Cold War were primarily political, while Text 2 argues that the causes were primarily economic.
   - Example: Text 1 argues that countries should invest in wind energy, while Text 2 argues that investing in wind energy is a waste.
2) They will agree on an issue, but for different reasons.
   - Example: Text 1 argues that a policy should be adopted because it benefits the economy, while Text 2 argues that it should be adopted for moral reasons.
3) They will discuss the same general topic, but focus on different aspects of that topic.
   - Example: Text 1 describes the history of the railroad, while Text 2 discusses the effects of the railroad on daily life.
   - Example: Text 1 describes the features of a piece of classical music, while Text 2 analyzes why the piece of music is so famous.
4) One passage discusses a topic in general, while the other discusses a specific example related to that topic.
   - Example: Text 1 discusses the importance of recycling, and Text 2 analyzes a recycling program in a specific community.

When asked to infer how the author of one passage (or a person mentioned in one passage) would respond to ideas in another, do the following:
   1) Read each passage and broadly consider the relationship between them in your own words.
   2) Identify what the first author says about the issue asked about in the question.
   3) Identify what the second author says about the issue asked about in the question.
   4) Analyze the relationship between the ideas. Consider what the authors (or people mentioned in a passage) agree or disagree about and why.

Sample 1

Text 1

Comedy does not belong in the workplace. Yes, everyone can benefit from smiling and laughing, especially during tense moments. But for the most part, interactions in traditional offices should be kept professional. Also, studies have shown that people are not as good at conveying and interpreting sarcastic remarks as they think. This could make for some awkward encounters between colleagues, undermining trust that is needed for effective teamwork.

Text 2

While workplace behavior should be professional and respectful, employees should not be afraid to be funny in the workplace. Stanford University researchers found that laughter can boost confidence and creativity in the workplace, making for a less stressful work environment. Laughter can even boost the immune system, and healthier employees are more likely to be present and engaged. It's no wonder many large corporations have hired comedy consultants and improvisation classes for their workers. Humor fosters camaraderie and leads to more innovative ideas.

Based on the texts, how would the author of Text 2 most likely react to the claim put forth in the last sentence of Text 1?
(A) By denying that there should be meaningful differences in how people interact in the workplace and in social settings.
(B) By insisting that the research shows disrespectful jokes are less likely to cause animosity between employees than disrespectful comments made without a humorous tone.
(C) By arguing that workplace humor can promote more effective and creative teamwork as long as the general professional environment is respectful.
(D) By countering that the majority of large corporations employ comedy consultants in order to maintain a competitive edge.

The first text takes a largely negative view of comedy in the workplace, concluding that it can hamper teamwork in part as a result of fostering distrust between employees. The second text takes a much more positive view of comedy, noting that it can boost productivity and creativity.

Choice A is incorrect. The second author only talks about comedy in the workplace, not social settings.

Choice B is not supported by the passage. While it notes the importance of being respectful, no mention of studies comparing the effects of disrespectful jokes to disrespectful literal statements is made.

Choice C matches our analysis. This author concludes that workplace humor can promote creativity and teamwork and acknowledges the importance of being respectful generally (hinting that this author agrees mean-spirited humor might not have the same positive impacts on employees). **This is the correct choice.**

Choice D is too extreme. While the passage notes that many companies have hired comedy consultants, we don't learn if this applies to the majority of large corporations.

Sample 2

Text 1
Yannick Donnadieu and colleagues ran computer simulations of global climate change 750 million years ago to try to determine what could have tipped the Earth into a "Snowball Earth" state, a supercooling scenario. They hypothesized that the breakup of the supercontinent Rodinia, promoted in part by eruptions of volcanic rocks, led to increased rainfall and thus increased weathering of rocks. Weathering could have a cooling effect, as more carbon dioxide was extracted from the air.

Text 2
Francis Macdonald and colleagues challenged the idea that weathering was responsible for the Snowball Earth. Though they acknowledged weathering could lead to the capture and storage of carbon dioxide, thus leading to a Snowball Earth, they expressed doubt that weathering would happen fast enough to lead to an overall net cooling of the planet: other feedbacks in the environment likely acted simultaneously and more quickly to warm it, such as volcanic activity. Instead, they argued that activity in one specific volcanic region known as the Franklin LIP likely led to the Snowball Earth, as eruptions in this sulfur-rich region could have led to sulfur eruptions redirecting solar energy and causing cooling.

Based on the texts, Macdonald would likely regard Donnadieu's hypothesis primarily as
(A) questionable, since the cooling effects of weathering would likely be outpaced by other activities that released carbon dioxide into the atmosphere.
(B) puzzling, since there is no evidence that weathering can lead to processes that capture and store atmosphere-warming carbon.
(C) nuanced, since it accounted for the ability of volcanic activity to have both warming and cooling effects on the environment.
(D) amateurish, since the models of climate change it ran were based on conjecture and speculation about an unproven continental breaking scenario.

Donnadieu believes rapid weathering led to the cooling that caused the Snowball Earth. Macdonald's team agrees that weathering can cause global cooling, but they doubt this would happen fast enough to offset the warming effects of other feedbacks in the environment. The right answer should relate to Macdonald's team disagreeing with the hypothesis because weathering was likely too slow to cause the Snowball Earth.

Choice A is correct and matches our prediction. While weathering can cause global cooling, Macdonald's team argued the cooling effects of weathering were likely outpaced by other activities that warmed the planet, meaning something else must have contributed to this cooling (since weathering is slow).

Choice B is wrong. While Macdonald's team would definitely disagree with Donnadieu's conclusions, that does not mean they would find them puzzling, or confusing. The team acknowledges weathering's potential to cause cooling: they just think it happened too slowly to cause the Snowball Earth.

Choice C is a trap. Macdonald's team would likely agree volcanic activity can have warming and cooling effects. Their agreement with this does not mean they find the hypothesis nuanced, or subtle and complex, which is a compliment. Overall, Macdonald's team disagrees with Donnadieu's hypothesis.

Choice D is too negative and another trap. Macdonald's team would disagree with Donnadieu's overall findings, but this is a far cry from accusing them of being amateurish (unprofessional) and unscientific in their methodology.

Text 1
Many small business owners are hesitant to delegate tasks to employees. Sometimes employers believe that if they don't have complete control over their businesses, mistakes will be made. In other instances, they believe that they must do virtually everything themselves to prove their expertise.

Text 2
Business owners must effectively delegate tasks to employees. Business owners who attempt to do everything themselves frequently delay projects because they simply do not have enough time in the day to achieve all their goals. Business owners who delegate work to others are in a better position to serve more customers and scale their businesses.

1. The author of Text 1 would most likely respond to the last sentence in Text 2 by arguing that
   (A) convincing certain business owners to entrust others with crucial responsibilities is likely going to be a challenge.
   (B) only employees that have experience running their own businesses are reliable.
   (C) the expertise of a business owner who works alone is more likely to attract a diverse consumer base.
   (D) the mistakes that employees will inevitably make counteract any benefits the business owner gains from delegating tasks.

Text 1
Employers should allow more employees to telecommute (work from home) when possible. Not only do such working arrangements save costs associated with running offices, but the flexibility of telecommuting jobs is also likely to drive company growth. Telecommuting options widen the pool of qualified applicants who have the potential to be productive and dedicated employees. Many capable prospective employees who have lifestyles that are not conducive to traveling into an office will be more inclined to apply for telecommuting positions.

Text 2
Employees who telecommute are less likely to feel engaged and emotionally satisfied in the workplace. If employees are not engaged, they will not be productive workers who are committed to their companies. Face-to-face interaction between workers adds value to companies.

2. The author of Text 2 would most likely respond to Text 1's claim that certain qualified employees are more likely to apply to telecommuting positions by saying that
   (A) there are no objective ways for determining if an employee does quality work.
   (B) the applicant pool will likely be expanded with weaker candidates.
   (C) even the most qualified applicants will be more productive in an office environment.
   (D) the educational credentials of employees who apply to telecommuting positions are likely to be weaker.

Text 1

Angela Duckworth's studies on grit argue for the importance of noncognitive factors—like passion and perseverance—in determining success. Many talented individuals who do not follow through on their commitments are ultimately outshined by their more persevering, grittier counterparts who were initially less skilled. While many educational institutions have embraced Duckworth's findings to pursue interventions that foster grit in their students, some critics claim that a hyperfocus on grit is a form of victim blaming that shifts lack of success on individual failures rather than on outside forces working against individuals; thus, efforts to enhance student achievement should address larger systemic forces that interact with student motivation.

Text 2

Professor Jai Mehta of the Harvard Graduate School of Education notes that though an emphasis on grit is a way of avoiding taking up larger questions of social justice, the bigger problem with grit proponents is that they misunderstand human motivation: people do not stop persevering at things because they lack motivation but because they find things not worth investing in. Thus, schools would be better served helping students develop purpose and passion by creating opportunities for them to have smaller mastery experiences, which will likely motivate them to persevere.

3. Based on the texts, Mehta would most likely say that the critics mentioned in the last sentence of Text 1

(A) have a much better understanding of motivation than do advocates of grit intervention programs.

(B) are largely correct in their assessment but overlook a more relevant problem with programs focused on promoting grit.

(C) do not have an adequate understanding of what grit is, leading them to have concerns that are unfounded.

(D) mean well in their advocacy for students, but fail to ponder solutions to improve student achievement.

Text 1

While nuclear power is a carbon-free energy source that is environmentally friendly, when accidents at nuclear power plants occur, the results are disastrous. Therefore, we should pause before we invest in nuclear power. In addition to the severe public health risks associated with nuclear power plants, nuclear power is also prohibitively expensive. Instead of investing more in nuclear power, clean renewable energy sources such as solar and wind energy should be used.

Text 2

Although certain costs associated with nuclear power plants are high, they pale in comparison to the damage done by carbon energy sources such as fossil fuels. In addition, there are some economic benefits associated with nuclear energy, such as reduced fuel and electricity costs. Nuclear power is a viable energy source that does not harm the environment. Unlike other forms of "clean energy," such as solar and wind energy, nuclear power is reliable: it is not dependent on weather conditions. Nuclear power is relatively safe, and the risk of accidents is decreasing thanks to enhanced safety measures.

4. The author of Text 2 would likely regard the author of Text 1's claim about "disastrous" results of accidents at nuclear power plants as

(A) misleading, since such accidents are rare and their impacts relatively minor when they do occur.

(B) alarmist, since there are adequate safeguards in place that minimize the chances of such accidents occurring.

(C) measured, because it balances the economic benefits of nuclear power against its impact on the environment.

(D) concerning, since it conflates the remedy to a common problem with the cause of the problem.

Text 1

Intraguild predation is thought to be commonplace in ecosystems. This occurs when an intraguild predator and an intraguild prey (an organism the intraguild predator consumes) both compete for the same pest. While empirical literature on this phenomenon is limited, most theorists argue that pest populations will be at their lowest when only the intraguild prey is present, as the intraguild predator would not be present to control the intraguild prey's populations. This should hold true regardless of whether the intraguild predator or prey is the superior natural enemy to the pests in question.

Text 2

Arne Janssen and colleagues decided to apply experimental techniques to better understand the effects of intraguild predation. Contrary to their expectations, intraguild predation did not increase pest populations. In many cases, the presence of the intraguild predator had either no effect— or even a negative effect —on pest populations. The team conceded that more research is needed to determine why their observed results failed to align with theoretical models.

5. Based on the texts, how would Janssen and colleagues likely react to the theory of the "theorists" mentioned in Text 1?

   (A) By acknowledging that Janssen's team's failure to find empirical support for the theory indicates a methodological flaw in their own study.

   (B) By suggesting that the theory is mostly accurate but requires minor tweaks, which future studies will confirm.

   (C) By admitting that while the theory the theorists advanced might seem plausible, it is not borne out by Janssen's team's findings.

   (D) By conjecturing that most experimental conditions would likely find support for it.

Text 1

The arts are a significant public good that benefit society in many ways. For example, economically, the arts can serve as engines of tourism, as evidenced by the number of people who visit cities with prominent museums and theatrical scenes. Educationally, arts education enriches the lives of young people, allowing them to foster their creativity and develop skills that will serve them in the workforce. Communities with vibrant art scenes are also more desirable places to live. For these reasons and more, governments should fund artistic endeavors that are unaffordable for most private individuals and organizations to subsidize adequately: the payoff in the form of increased taxes, tourism, and small business patronage will more than make up for the investment.

Text 2

Nobody doubts the benefits that arts can have on people and communities. However, with limited resources to spend, it is unclear why the government should prioritize funding the arts when there are more pressing issues to deal with, such as healthcare, environmental matters, and national security. If people really care about patronizing the arts, private funding would be enough to accomplish this. For example, restaurants might hire musicians that will draw in more diners. If the arts are not being funded, maybe there is just not the demand for art that public funding advocates believe there is.

6. The author of Text 1 would most likely object to the claim made in the last sentence of Text 2 on the grounds that it
   (A) overlooks the possibility that funding artistic endeavors will render increased funding for other sectors of society unnecessary due to art's broad societal benefits.
   (B) conflates a financial inability to fund artistic ventures with a lack of interest in consuming the artistic products of such ventures.
   (C) insinuates that only people who are financially well off are entitled to reaping the benefits of artistic pursuits.
   (D) feigns ignorance to the economic benefits that a vibrant art scene can generate for state and local governments.

Text 1

Conventional wisdom long held that Neanderthals developed modern tools solely through contact with modern humans. Paleoanthropologists traditionally believed that Neanderthals were relatively unintelligent and thick-skulled, and thus outcompeted by modern humans who arrived in Europe from Africa. Neanderthals were seen as scavengers who could only create the most rudimentary of tools and who were incapable of thinking symbolically. They were likely absorbed by modern humans and have contributed between 1% and 4% of their DNA to people in Asia and Europe.

Text 2

In research published in *Journal of Archaeological Method and Theory,* anthropologist Julien Riel-Salvatore maintained that Neanderthals were capable of creating, adapting, and evolving technology of their own without the assistance of modern humans. His conclusion was based on the discovery of tool artifacts similar to those used by modern humans—such as projectile points, ochre, and bone tools— from areas of Italy believed to be geographically separated from modern humans.

7. Based on the texts, how would Riel-Salvatore most likely respond to the "conventional wisdom" as presented in Text 1?

(A) By denying that modern humans and Neanderthals ever had any direct physical interactions with one another.

(B) By disputing the assumption that Neanderthals lacked the intelligence to produce cultural artifacts reminiscent of those created by modern humans.

(C) By emphasizing the importance of tool creation in both early Neanderthal and modern societies and downplaying the importance of symbolic rituals.

(D) By conceding that Neanderthals lacked meaningful intelligence but noting that intelligence was not a prerequisite to creating relatively advanced technology.

Text 1

In the 1980s, scientists discovered that sequenceable DNA could be recovered from museum specimens and fossils. This led to the exciting idea that extinct species could be brought back to life, a phenomenon known as de-extinction. Advances in DNA sequencing technologies and genome editing tools mean that reconstructing the genomes of extinct species is plausible. The company Colossal Biosciences is working to revive the thylacine, a wolf-like creature that went extinct due to human activity in the early twentieth century. This might be accomplished by using genetic editing technology on the genome of the thylacine's closest living relative, the dunnart, with the goal of releasing a viable and diverse population of thylacines in the wild.

Text 2

The idea of resurrecting wooly mammoths, the dodo bird, and the Christmas Island rat may evoke awe and wonder, but proponents of the de-extinction must be sober-minded about what these efforts would entail. De-extinction programs may give the general population false hope that threatened biodiversity is easy to solve. With limited financial and intellectual resources to spare, lofty programs that aim to restore extinct species might detract from efforts to help living species that are in danger of becoming extinct. Advanced genomic technologies would be better served helping endangered species. Even if we could bring extinct species back, would they truly be able to thrive in the habitat they deserve?

8. Based on the texts, what would the author of Text 2 most likely say about the author of the project to restore the thylacines discussed in Text 1?

   (A) It is reasonable since the efforts to restore thylacines will maximize the affordances of advanced genetics technologies to protect threatened and endangered species.

   (B) It is a malicious attempt to divert funding from endangered species who will almost surely go extinct because of projects such as these.

   (C) It is unexpected given that most scientists understand the complexity of the problem the project seeks to rectify.

   (D) It is a misguided and wasteful effort that is not in the best interests of preserving biodiversity.

Text 1

Scientists in Switzerland led by Johan Auwerk found that they could use gene therapy to transform mice into "super mice" who run at extraordinary speeds. They did this by creating a virus that knocked out a gene that makes the protein nuclear receptor corepressor 1 (NCoR1) in mice's muscles. Treated mice gained muscle mass without needing extra food to be sustained. Auwerk believes his study might pave the way for research on targeted gene therapies that can invigorate the muscles of humans, including the elderly and those with muscle disorders.

Text 2

Many athletes will seek out anything that can give them a competitive edge in their sports, whether it be certain nutritional supplements, specialized equipment, or tailored training regimens. While scientists in Switzerland have come across a promising way to increase muscle size and speed in mice (gene therapy blocking the production of protein NCoR1), human athletes should not try to enhance their performance by illegally procuring interventions that target NCoR1. No trials have been conducted in humans, and it is possible that side effects of drugs targeting NCoR1 can be serious, as this protein serves other vital functions throughout the body.

9. Based on the texts, how would the author of Text 2 likely regard the suggestions for future applications of interventions targeting NCoR1 in humans discussed in Text 1?

(A) With approval, since helping those with muscle weakness is a more honorable purpose than helping athletes enhance their performance.

(B) With disdain, since such interventions would cause unintended side effects.

(C) With skepticism, since more research must be done to determine the safety of such interventions in humans.

(D) With resignation, since people will generally seek out risky but alluring novelties that may improve their quality of life.

Text 1

A study led by Kevin France of the University of Colorado concluded that planets orbiting close to the most numerous and long-lasting stars in our galaxy, red dwarfs, are likely unsuitable for life. This finding was based on the study of one star, Barnard's star: this star released scorching solar flares that likely damaged the atmospheres of planets close by it, rendering the planets unlikely to sustain life.

Text 2

There has long been concern that solar flares, among other factors, might render planets located near red dwarfs inhospitable. These flares might extinguish any life that develops and destroy atmospheres. Yet a study led by Ekaterina Ilin has found evidence that the impact of flares on planet habitability might be weaker than previously thought. A study of four red dwarf stars found that many of the most damaging flares strike planets at an angle instead of directly, diminishing their impact on habitability. Still, the study's researchers did concede that ultraviolet radiation and even high-impact particles from solar flares could still present challenges for planets and that more research is needed.

10. Based on the texts, how would Ilin and colleagues likely regard the conclusion of France?

(A) As groundbreaking, because solar flares do have potential to wipe out atmospheres of planets.

(B) As premature, because preliminary evidence suggests the damaging impact of solar flares from red dwarfs can be minimized in some cases.

(C) As fraudulent, since France's study did not use a scientifically rigorous sample.

(D) As unexpected, because it has been long established that solar flares hit planets at angles rather than directly.

Text 1

Basalt is a volcanic rock that forms when lava with a high concentration of mafic minerals solidifies after it cools. According to conventional wisdom, massive magma eruptions forming floods of basalt lava occur in low-pressure regions with thin continental tectonic plates. The low-pressure conditions allow for the melting of the hot mantle, generating vast quantities of magma. Trace element compositions of erupted magma show evidence of magma formation under low-pressure conditions. However, scientists cannot explain the discovery of flood basalt zones in regions with thick tectonic plates that seemingly resulted from magma formed under high-pressure conditions.

Text 2

A team led by Dr. Arturo Luttinen hypothesized that the melting of exceptionally hot mantles can lead to high-pressure magmas with chemical compositions comparable to those of low-pressure magmas. A computer simulation using geothermal modeling confirmed this hypothesis. For instance, the element garnet is consumed under high-pressure conditions with very high temperatures, and it can survive in low-pressure conditions when the mantle composition is different. Thus, the team notes that trace chemical compositions are "unreliable messengers of magma generation depth" when mantle temperature and composition are unaccounted for: flood basalts can form in thick tectonic plate regions and under high-pressure conditions if the mantle is exceptionally hot.

11. Based on the texts, how would the author of Text 2 respond to the "conventional wisdom" in Text 1?

(A) By stating that it is partially grounded in a misconception about the significance of certain chemical signatures in flood basalt regions.

(B) By recommending more geologists use computer simulations to reconcile long-standing debates about how volcanoes function.

(C) By suggesting their own findings clarify how garnet allows magma to adapt differentially to high-pressure and low-pressure conditions.

(D) By asserting that it fails to recognize that voluminous magma eruptions necessitate thick tectonic plates that are melted at extremely high temperatures.

Text 1

Conventional wisdom holds that farming was invented in the Near East over 10,000 years ago and then was spread to other places. Most research has centered around the Fertile Crescent, areas that include many modern Middle Eastern countries such as Israel, Palestine, Turkey, and Syria. Hunter gatherers collected seeds from a variety of wild cereals and legumes to produce foods that were easy to harvest, such as wheat, barley, and lentils.

Text 2

Archaeologists Nicholas Conard and Simone Riehl discovered evidence of farming in Chogha Golan in Iran, which is much farther east than the Fertile Crescent. There, they found evidence of plant processing in the form of mortars, pestles, and grounding stone. Radiocarbon dating confirmed that the people of Chogha Golan began cultivating many legumes as early as 11,500 years ago. The researchers concluded that farming was inevitable after the Ice Age and arose independently in multiple regions.

12. How would Conard and Riehl likely react to the conventional wisdom discussed in Text 1?

(A) By disputing the idea that the development of farming spread outwardly from a single focal point.

(B) By questioning the assumption that the end of the Ice Age prompted the rise of agricultural methods.

(C) By asserting that the Fertile Crescent's agricultural sophistication was dependent on assistance from civilizations farther east.

(D) By suggesting that the development of farming was a linear process with clearly defined stages.

Text 1

Neuroanatomist Suzana Herculano-Houzel argued that the dinosaur *Tyrannosaurus rex* might not be as dimwitted as had previously been thought. This is based on findings that suggest the dinosaur may have had a comparable number of brain cells (neurons) to modern monkeys, about 3 billion to be exact. This conclusion was based on data from living birds and reptiles, which Herculano-Houzel extrapolated towards dinosaurs with scaled up skull sizes. If the number of brain cells reflects intelligence, Herculano-Houzel argued that these giants might have been "endowed with flexible cognition, and thus [are] more magnificent than previously thought," possibly possessing the ability to utilize tools.

Text 2

Many scientists were skeptical of claims that *Tyrannosaurus rex* may have possessed monkey-like intelligence. Zoologist Kai Caspar cautions against making inferences about animal intelligence based on sheer brain size. For example, Caspar notes that crows have small brains relative to their bodies and fewer neurons than baboons, yet crows perform better on cognitive tasks. Instead, synaptic connections (connections between neurons) might matter more for intelligence than brain size or the number of neural cells.

13. Based on the texts, Caspar would likely criticize Herculano-Houzel for
    (A) failing to include mammals in the data collection process that involved studying live birds and reptiles in her study.
    (B) relying on statistically weak extrapolations to draw conclusions about the number of brain cells in *Tyrannosaurus rex.*
    (C) ignoring the fact that skull size does not necessarily equate to brain size or mass when estimating the number of brain cells in *Tyrannosaurus rex.*
    (D) drawing an ambitious conclusion about *Tyrannosaurus rex*'s capabilities based on a fallible indicator of intelligence.

The first passage is adapted from Federalist Paper 78, and the second paper is adapted from Brutus XV ("Anti-Federalist Paper" 15). Both passages were written in the 1780s before the ratification of the United States Constitution. Both passages address the power of the judicial branch (the courts).

Text 1

Whoever attentively considers the different departments of power must perceive that, in a government in which they are separated from each other, the judiciary, from the nature of its functions, will always be the least dangerous to the political rights of the Constitution; because it will be least in a capacity to annoy or injure them. The executive not only dispenses the honors but holds the sword of the community. The legislature (Congress, law-making body) not only commands the purse but prescribes the rules by which the duties and rights of every citizen are to be regulated. The judiciary, on the contrary, has no influence over either the sword or the purse; no direction either of the strength or of the wealth of the society, and can take no active resolution whatsoever. It may truly be said to have neither FORCE nor WILL but merely judgment; and must ultimately depend upon the aid of the executive arm even for the efficacy of its judgment.

Text 2

The power of this court is in many cases superior to that of the legislature. The supreme court then has a right, independent of the legislature, to give a construction to the constitution and every part of it, and there is no power provided in this system to correct their construction or do it away. If, therefore, the legislature passes any laws, inconsistent with the sense the judges put upon the constitution, they will declare it void; and therefore in this respect their power is superior to that of the legislature.

14. The author of Text 2 would likely argue the author of Text 1's assertion that the courts have the power of "merely judgment"
    (A) understates the undue influence that courts have on the political system.
    (B) exaggerates the strength of the judiciary relative to the other branches of government.
    (C) accurately reflects the scope of judicial powers.
    (D) fails to recognize the potential for the executive to ignore the judiciary's rulings.

Text 1

The film *Everything Everywhere All At Once*—an action-packed comedy drama about a dimension-hopping family— was undoubtedly a pop culture juggernaut that was commendable for centering an Asian American family. While it received a record number of Oscars at the Academy Awards, some critics lamented that the film was "too sincere" and a bit "heavy-handed" with its themes. Although most critics agreed that it was a fun film, some were skeptical that it rose to the level of a high-brow film that is typically honored with "serious" awards.

Text 2

Everything Everywhere All At Once was certainly a bit stylistically different from a typical Academy Award Best Picture winner, but the film's "wackiness" and frenetic pacing do not detract from its intellectual worthiness. Although some of the films it beat out explored its themes with more subtlety, the core emotional message of *Everything Everywhere All At Once* is highly resonant and presented with deftness.

15. The author of Text 2 would likely respond to the critics in Text 1 by
    (A) conceding that *Everything Everywhere All At Once* would have been a much more effective film had it explored more complex themes with greater subtlety.
    (B) disagreeing that *Everything Everywhere All At Once* had zany elements that distinguish it from similarly acclaimed films.
    (C) agreeing that *Everything Everywhere All At Once* is less impressive than other films that have won Academy Awards but insisting that it should still be regarded as a classic.
    (D) acknowledging that *Everything Everywhere All At Once* clearly has stylistic differences from some other well-regarded modern films but that it deserves to be treated seriously as a work with cinematic merit nonetheless.

Text 1 is adapted from Jefferson Davis's 1861 speech "On Withdrawing from the Union." Text 2 is adapted from Waitman Willey's 1861 speech at the Virginia State Secession Convention. The first passage discusses the secession of Mississippi from the Union prior to the Civil War. The second excerpt discusses secession in general.

Text 1

Secession belongs to a different class of remedies. It is to be justified upon the basis that the States are sovereign. A State finding herself in the condition in which Mississippi has judged she is, in which her safety requires that she should provide for the maintenance of her rights out of the Union, surrenders all the benefits (and they are known to be many), deprives herself of the advantages (they are known to be great), severs all the ties of affection (and they are close and enduring), which have bound her to the Union; and thus divesting herself of every benefit, taking upon herself every burden, she claims to be exempt from any power to execute the laws of the United States within her term.

Text 2

If the doctrine of the right of a State to secede at her own good will and pleasure be true, then, sir, we may engage in a war, and in the very crisis of the country's extremity, a State may retire from the Union, and out of danger; and if she be indeed independent and sovereign when she goes, may form a treaty of alliance with the enemies of the Government. Or she may wait until the war is concluded-a war in which the blood of her confederates may have been shed in defending her soil-and when the enemy is repelled, when the debt incurred by the war is resting on the country, politely make her bow, retire from the Union, and leave the remaining States to pay the debt incurred in defending her soil, and in vindicating her honor? Can it be possible that Washington, and Madison, and Franklin*, and the other sages of the Revolution, have organized a Government upon such an absurd basis as this?

*The listed people were Founding Fathers of America who helped craft the structure of its government

16. The author of Text 2 would likely characterize Mississippi's decision to withdraw from the Union as
    (A) rational due to its inevitable economic collapse.
    (B) motivated by legitimate threats to its safety.
    (C) justified under the doctrine of states' rights.
    (D) inconsistent with the intentions of the Constitution's frame

Text 1

In Lorraine Hansberry's seminal play *A Raisin in The Sun*, she explores many heavy themes, including the challenges of achieving the American Dream and the importance of fighting against racial discrimination. Some critics, believing Hansberry sought to reject the American Dream outright, noted what they saw as clunky contradictions, unintentional ironies, and thematic conflicts in her work.

Text 2

Lorraine Hansberry does not reject the American Dream in *A Raisin in the* Sun; rather, she embraces it while lamenting its incomplete realization. She does advocate for ethnic awareness of the Black identity, but she sees this as compatible with interracial harmony. Hansberry's skillful use of deliberate irony allows her to make an incisive social commentary that helps unify thematic elements that might seem to clash superficially.

17. The author of Text 2 would most likely argue that critics mentioned in Text 1
    (A) unfairly nitpick at subtle contradictions in Hansberry's work while neglecting its more socially empowering elements.
    (B) fail to appreciate *A Raisin in the Sun's* ironic nuances as compatible with its thematic consistency.
    (C) incorrectly interpret a play that is meant to be taken literally from an ironic lens.
    (D) typically underestimate the capacity of playwrights to employ ironic devices as a vehicle for social commentary.

Text 1

Streaming services allow music listeners to have access to millions of songs for a small fee so they don't have to individually purchase CDs or albums. Some artists, such as Taylor Swift, have lamented that music streaming services have done a disservice to artists, as the price of music in a streaming model does not reflect its worth. Indeed, music sales revenue did decline steeply as digital music grew in popularity.

Text 2

Streaming revenues have been increasing in recent years and are beginning to make up for some of the lost music industry profits associated with digital streaming. Evidence is emerging that even customers who stream music are still willing to buy songs and albums by traditional avenues. Beyond this, streaming makes music more accessible and drives concert sales, which Hugh Zehr of the University of Iowa argues may eventually offset losses in revenue from reduced music ownership. Marketing costs to fledgling artists also decrease as their music can garner attention more easily, while superstar artists like Taylor Swift can use their labels to negotiate better royalty deals.

18. Based on the texts, Zehr would most likely state that the concerns voiced by Taylor Swift in Text 1 are

(A) highly unreasonable, as concert ticket sales are more expensive than album purchases.

(B) extremely prophetic, as the music industry's declining revenues as a result of digitization are likely to be more extreme than other industries' profit losses as a result of digitization.

(C) somewhat overblown, because promising evidence suggests the losses in revenue as a result of streaming are beginning to be offset as the music industry adapts.

(D) completely hypocritical, as superstar artists who overestimate their value will continue to make a living.

Text 1

Some acting schools stress the importance of repeatedly generating specific emotions. For example, they might have students conjure up memories from their own experiences or those of others they have read about in books in order to produce a compelling emotional performance. As actors advance through their training, they will become more adept at summoning authentic emotions on demand.

Text 2

Training actors to summon up repeatable emotions on demand is not necessarily productive and, if anything, it can be traumatic (especially if it involves drawing on unpleasant memories). While being in tune with one's emotions is essential to quality performances, actors should not let a hyperfocus on emotion interfere with the action of a scene. Instead, actors should focus on studying the script. Only then can actors give more spontaneous, authentic performances that are grounded in the imaginary circumstances in which they must perform.

19. The author of Text 2 would likely argue that the "authentic emotions" cited in Text 1

(A) regrettably require that actors reflect on past personal traumas in order to be accessed.

(B) prevent spontaneous interactions between actors that allow their characters to come off as less affected.

(C) are more likely to be conveyed in performances when actors engage in meticulous textual analysis.

(D) delay the pacing of action that brings scenes to life.

Text 1

Increasing employee wages is often thought to increase corporate profits, as the extra money spent on paying employees can be offset in the form of decreased costs associated with turnover and training new hires, increased employee engagement and productivity, and increased sales as a result of positive brand recognition from appreciative customers. An economics student ran a computer simulation and found that modestly increasing wages at a certain bank would actually wipe out corporate profits in a three-month period.

Text 2

While the initial investment associated with rising wages can lower corporate profits initially, combined with strategic business practices, raising wages should increase long-term profits for most companies. A study of a big box retailer found that after it increased its wages and benefits for employees, the company saw higher sales per square root than did its direct competitors over a 16-year period and had a turnover rate that was near zero, well below the industry average.

20. How would the author of Text 2 likely respond to the findings of the economics student in Text 1?
    (A) The author would likely recommend that the student run simulations examining the short-term profits at banks in different markets.
    (B) The author would likely claim that banks' profits are uniquely vulnerable to budget increases in a way not relevant to most industries.
    (C) The author would likely urge the student to analyze if the decrease in bank profits would persist over a more extended timeframe.
    (D) The author would likely predict that corporate profits for the bank would continue to decline for many years.

Drill 1

1. **B.** The text makes clear that one purpose of the organization is to hire Native American artists, a group who is often overlooked (unnoticed) by the general public, giving them the chance to be more economically self-sufficient.

2. **A.** The narrator's experience eating meat for the first time caused her to experience a moral conflict. On the one hand, she enjoyed it and the event was symbolic of barriers breaking down between her culture and the West. On the other hand, she felt as if she had betrayed her grandmother by violating a cultural tradition.

3. **C.** Sara is a skilled storyteller who enraptures her audience. The descriptive details about how she gives her stories life supports the broader point that she enjoys telling stories and was good at telling them: "Sara not only could tell stories, but she adored telling them."

4. **C.** The main idea is that Brown rejected a mimetic (imitative) approach to art and experimented with abstractions. The two examples of paintings discussed illustrate the broader point about how she painted abstractly without faithfully recreating the scenes she was reproducing.

5. **B.** The text makes clear Quijote entertained those around him during his adventures: "Gradually, his exploits became known all over the countryside, and there were few who had not heard of that flower of chivalry, Don Quixote de la Mancha."

6. **D.** The passage describes way that Marlow was different from the other sailors: "He was the only man of us who still 'followed the sea.' The worst that could be said of him was that he did not represent his class." While most sailors were content to lead more sedentary lives, Marlow was a wanderer.

7. **A.** The responsibilities of tribal libraries have changed over time (they adapted to the digital age by taking on new functions), but they remain important in preserving cultural information.

8. **A.** Although the speaker seems to experience some struggles and homesickness during the chilly winters of the North, the last stanza makes clear that he loves how the spring transforms the North: "When Spring has shed upon the earth her charm/You'll love the Northland wreathed in golden smiles/By the miraculous sun turned glad and warm." In other words, spring brings positive changes to the North that people who come North will love. The description of the sun as "miraculous," "glad," and "warm" suggests his positive feelings for Northern springs.

9. **C.** Edward has more modest ambitions for himself, only wanting "domestic comfort" and "the quiet of private life." This is at odds with the aspirations his mother and sister have for him, who wanted him to distinguish himself in his career.

10. **C.** The baobab trees are "dying prematurely at alarmingly higher rates." In other words, they are dying before the end of their lifespans.

11. **A.** John relies on Alexandra for her resourcefulness and good judgment. She is extremely insightful (perceptive) when it comes to agricultural matters, as evidenced by this statement: "It was Alexandra who could always tell about what it had cost to fatten each steer, and who could guess the weight of a hog before it went on the scales closer than John Bergson himself."

12. **D.** The main point is that even though one can get demoralized when failing to achieve goals, we are ultimately better off setting more ambitious goals, as doing so helps us achieve more than we otherwise would have with more modest goals.

13. **B**. The fossil from the early Late Cretaceous period was the "first definitive thyreophoran species from this region (Patagonian region of South America)." This means the geographic range (location where thyreophoran species roamed) was wider than previously known.

14. **A.** Sister Carrie is "ambitious to gain in material things." In other words, she desires acquiring tangible possessions.

15. **B.** Emily Dickinson makes clear that she is anonymous ("I'm Nobody! Who are you?") and wishes to remain that way ("Don't tell! they'd advertise – you know!"). She says it is "dreary" to be "Somebody." She suggests public figures are exposed like frogs. Overall, Dickinson suggests a private life is preferable to one as public figure.

16. **C.** The narrator indicates sports served a pragmatic (practical, or real-world) purpose: "indeed, we practiced only what we expected to do when grown." Indian boys were trained in tasks they were expected to master for adulthood.

17. **C.** The main idea is that years after the existence of Higgs particles was proposed, scientists were finally able to prove that they existed by using the LHC.

18. **D.** We learn that Little Chandler puts a lot of care into his personal appearance and personal grooming: he takes great care of his hair, mustache, and nails.

19. **C.** When the girl suggests Shchupkin cannot be a writer based on his poor handwriting, he counters that handwriting is not relevant to being a writer, citing that Nekrassov is an author with bad handwriting. Thus, handwriting should not be the basis on which to judge his professional capabilities (his skills as a writer).

20. **B.** Thea and Ray disagree about the extent to which individuals are responsible for their own successes and failures. Thea believes the responsibility lies on oneself ("Everybody's up against it for himself, succeeds or fails—himself"), while Ray believes outside forces play a big role in determining one's success ("But when you look at it another way, there are a lot of halfway people in this world who help the winners win, and the failers fail").

21. **C.** The studies of cool flames cannot be studied as effectively on Earth because the buoyancy of Earth causes the fuel droplets to lose their symmetry quickly, while the buoyancy of space allows droplets to retain their symmetry.

22. **A.** Dickinson says, "And sore must be the storm/That could abash the little Bird." This means it takes an unusually powerful storm to defeat a bird. Since hope is being compared to a bird ("the thing with feathers"), the implication is that hope, like a bird, is formidable (strong) in the face of challenging circumstances.

23. **D.** White Fang learns to tolerate the master's other dogs and Matt because that is what his master expects of him. He only let Matt drive him because he sensed that was his master's will. Overall, we get the impression that White Fang puts his master's needs ahead of all others and bends to his will. White Fang merely tolerates other entities whom his master wants him to interact with civilly.

24. **A.** While Tillie thinks all the Kronborgs are worthy, she knew Thea was different from the others and special. She imagines lofty possibilities for Thea's life. Overall, we get the impression that Tillie holds Thea in high esteem.

25. **A.** The researchers concluded that surprised infants were better at learning the ball squeaked based on the amount of time they spent looking at the ball. They looked at the ball longer than the infants who were not surprised. This suggested they learned to associate the squeak with the ball.

26. **B**. When reflecting on the past, the speaker feels sad. But when he thinks of his friend, he feels comforted ("But if the while I think on thee, dear friend,
All losses are restored and sorrows end").

Drill 2

1. **B.** The excerpt "Sometimes if we'd stop to think/And count the good deeds we do/ To help those on Poverty's brink/We'd find them to be few" suggests that if we stop to reflect on the good we do help others, we would find that these acts are small in number. Thus, we do not maximize the good we are capable of doing (we do not do as much good as we possibly can).

2. **B.** The student predicted plants grown in soil with lime (the more alkaline soil) would see more growth. If the plants grown *without* lime grew taller, this would weaken the student's conclusion.

3. **D.** The table shows in the last row that support in District 4 stood at 25%.

4. **C.** We are looking for a choice that shows a large difference in high temperatures or large difference in low temperatures between two cities. C shows a large difference in low temperature between two cities.

5. **B.** The statement "Your friend is your needs answered" suggests that a friend meets people's needs (solves their problems).

6. **C.** The number of farms Oregon had in this industry was around 2,800, which is between 2,000 and 3,000. It is the only accurate choice.

7. **A.** If dogs are largely incapable of hunting marine animals that would not have been accessible to them by hunting and there is evidence the dogs consumed the marine animals anyway, this could suggest humans who caught marine animals fed them to dogs, supporting the hypothesis.

8. **D.** We would not expect there to be iron on the moon if the moon came from the Earth's mantle, and we would expect the moon to be less dense since the mantle is less dense than the core. However, evidence of differences in composition for materials deep below the moon's surface might suggest the moon's origin is at least in part from a body that did not come from Earth.

9. **C.** If certain types of architecture that appeared outside of the Olmec territory predate similar architecture by the Olmecs, this would support the idea that the Olmec was not the mother (originator) of culture. Perhaps different Mesoamerican cultures influenced one another.

10. **D.** The lines "A man's right to speak does not depend upon where he was born or upon his color. The simple quality of manhood is the solid basis of the right – and there let it rest forever" show that Douglass did not believe one's right to free speech is contingent, or dependent, on one's life circumstances. All people have that right regardless of their race or geographic origin.

11. **C.** To prove the point that ablation rates vary for any given element in different types of dust, we need data that shows the same element has a different ablation rate in a different dust type. The given data point in the question stem is about silicon in slow-moving JFC dust, so the right answer should show a different ablation rate for silicon in a fast-moving OOC or HTC dust, as choice C shows.

12. **C.** The fact that a majority of rural counties in some regions but not others saw rural population loss supports the idea that some regions were more susceptible to rural population loss than others. The graph shows that more than 50% (half) of rural counties in the Northeast and Midwest saw population loss, but less than 50% of those in the South did.

13. **D.** D is true (output levels were highest for both Japan and the United States in 2011). It also supports the point that output has increased in both countries.

14. **C.** Comparing the data from 2006 to 2010 shows that both countries saw a dramatic increase in the percentage of households with internet access. However, it also makes clear that the rate of increase was very different. Though there was only a 3 percentage point difference between France and Spain in 2006, this difference was 16 points by 2010, showing that the percentage of households with internet in France increased more dramatically by 2010. By 2015, the percentage of households with internet access was similar in both countries.

15. **A.** If the curator had been successful in her aims, then more artwork by Latin American artists should have been featured at the museum, as choice A shows.

16. **B.** If fossils of dinosaurs were found over a wider geographic range than fossils of known ectotherms, this might provide evidence that endothermy was the trait that enabled these dinosaurs to roam over greater distances, as endothermy might allow organisms to be more active.

17. **A.** A is the only choice that explicitly mentions Picasso using his artwork itself as a medium of expressing his political beliefs, namely his opposition to certain fascist and dictatorial regimes.

18. **D.** If sea urchins make pits even when they have adequate pits to provide shelter, this suggests there is some other reason they make pits. Perhaps the act of making pits serves a biological benefit to sea urchins, lending credence to the student's hypothesis.

19. **C.** If plants not under attack connected to ones who are under attack **do** produce chemicals to ward off insects and plants not under attack whose connection to attacked plants is severed **do not** produce such chemicals, this would support the hypothesis that there is a communication network between plants in which they are connected by the fungi. If the connection is severed, plants not under attack will not be warned to start producing chemicals.

20. **C.** Choice C is the only quote that both describes the natural environment and makes clear the narrator feels deeply connected to it: "I was something that lay under the sun and felt it, like the pumpkins, and I did not want to be anything more. I was entirely happy." The narrator felt at one with nature.

21. **B.** If advancements in AI allow it to take over certain tasks while allowing humans to focus on other tasks that are best done by humans, this shows that human workers are unlikely to be replaced (though the nature of their jobs may change).

22. **D.** If the researchers are correct, subjects in the competition condition should pay more attention, which is suggested by faster reaction times. Choice D shows that reaction times were slower in the self-condition, meaning people likely paid less attention in this condition (and thus were faster and paid more attention in the competition condition).

23. **C.** If students who were placed in a condition designed to increase their feelings of empathy did indeed act more altruistically by helping Carol more, this would support Batson's argument that empathy prompts helping behavior.

24. **A.** Ripple's hypothesis predicts that wolf reintroduction decreases coyote populations. If there is evidence that wolves can have positive effects on coyote populations, this would undermine Ripple's hypothesis.

25. **B.** If it is true that declining seal and sea otter populations are associated with increased sea urchin populations and sea urchins feed on kelp, this might support the hypothesis by suggesting the higher urchin populations led to more kelp being eaten.

26. **D.** Choice D supports the finding because it gives an example of two countries with notably different urbanization rates that nonetheless had very similar economic growth rates.

27. **A.** If it is true that more education is positively associated with voting, then we would expect more educated voters to vote at higher rates than less educated voters who are otherwise similar. The fact that when gender is held constant, more educated voters vote at higher rates, as seen in the graph, supports this point.

28. **B.** In both empathy conditions, people helped more if there was a high personal cost to not helping. However, the fact that high-empathy individuals with little to lose by not helping still helped more than low-empathy individuals who had more to personally lose by not helping supports the idea that empathy can be a powerful motivator.

29. **B.** In order to weaken the traditional view, we need evidence that voters who vote in schools are more likely to vote for education funding when other factors are held constant (controlled for). Choice B is the only choice that accomplishes this. Even among voters who live near a school, when other factors are controlled for, those who voted in a school were more likely to support the tax, hinting that the venue may have impacted their votes.

30. **C.** A detail about an exhibit that features Latin American and Latino artists not affected by European traditions would best strengthen the claim that curators are countering the Eurocentric narrative that European art influenced Latin American and Latino art. Choice C best illustrates this by mentioning Latin American artists uninfluenced by European traditions.

31. **A.** Choice A best support the idea that there are interpersonal conflicts between artists by highlighting that artists often argue with each other.

32. **D.** It females prefer male scrub jays with the same beak length, this would lead to more divergence between the subspecies over time. If the male oak forest scrub jays' beaks have gotten shorter relative to those of male pine forest scrub jays, this would provide evidence that the species is differentiating.

33. **B.** Choice B makes clear that Harold has a pleasant appearance (he is handsome) but hints at his unpleasant behavior (he was forgiven of everything, suggesting he acted in unpleasant ways). The fact that his being handsome had been "trouble all along" hints at a longstanding pattern of bad behavior for which those around him constantly forgave him.

34. **D.** If it were found that galaxies without dark matter existed, this would undermine the idea that dark matter is essential scaffolding that is essential to galaxy formation (if it is essential, we would assume all galaxies would have dark matter).

35. **D.** Quote D, which seems to praise Joan for her political idealism and as example of women's heroism is evidence of the type of positive characterization (her characterization has a feminist hero) about Joan of Arc of which the student complains.

36. **D.** When Lady Macbeth says that all the perfumes of Arabia will not sweeten her hand and that there is blood on it, she shows that she feels remorseful. She has done something so horrible that there is no becoming "clean" from what she did.

37. **C.** The fact that among frogs with exposure to UVB, those at higher altitudes seemed to have less DNA damage (as indicated by lower MNE values) supports the hypothesis that higher-altitude frogs have mechanisms that protect them against DNA damage.

38. **C.** The fact that Ancient breeds (which are most like wolves) took longer to look at humans and spent less time gazing at them supports the prediction that these breeds would show less spontaneous gazing towards humans.

39. **A.** For every prize amount, people in the rival condition took more risks, showing they were less risk averse (less opposed to taking risks). This would support the prediction that people are more likely to take risks against rivals.

40. **C.** Potatoes were not expected to grow better in wood ash. The fact that they grew slightly more in wood ash would be surprising.
41. **B.** General economic uncertainty was higher than monetary policy uncertainty in 2018, as can be seen by the higher bar for general uncertainty. In 2023, the bar for monetary policy was much higher than that for general economic uncertainty. This shows that general uncertainty need not reflect uncertainty about specific economic measures.
42. **D.** If students in the control group scored lower, this would support the idea that passive learning was less effective at helping students learn the material.
43. **D.** D supports the ideas that the orcas are becoming different over time. If this trend continues, the subspecies will likely diverge into different species.
44. **A.** A shows that changing the proxy for tool reduction produced different results for the same measure (the measure being spurs per interface value). This supports the hypothesis that the proxy used matters in judging Weedman's hypothesis.
45. **C.** There are 39 plays attributed to Shakespeare shown on the table. If it is true he possibly collaborated with playwrights on other plays, this would mean the actual number of plays he wrote is greater than what the table shows. Thus, the table shows the bare minimum number of plays to which Shakespeare could have contributed.
46. **C.** That all plants grown with salt grew less than the control group did showed salt stunted the growth. That the plants grown with salt and additional species (groups 3 and 4) grew more than the one only grown in salt (group 2) shows that additional species can minimize the stunting impact of salt on growth.
47. **D.** The speaker asks the wind to scatter his words, or spread his ideas to the world.
48. **C.** If mitochondrial DNA only reveals information about maternal DNA, this leaves open the possibility that Minoans descended in part from large populations of Egyptian men.
49. **D.** That the rain is "dripping" in D suggests the storm is subsiding. Since the rain is compared to golden honey, which is sweet, beautiful, and healing, it is logical the student might infer the poem suggests that tumultuous experiences can have beautiful endings and lead to healing.

Drill 3

1. **A.** If most of the cost decreases were from printing and distributing, this suggests other parts of the writing process (artwork, writing, editing) were less impacted by cost decreases.
2. **C.** The passage suggests the method Bakker's team used to decide the specimen was an adult (analysis of bone sutures) is not completely reliable, since there is variation in how this process occurs between species. Thus, the fact that the bones appeared fully fused cannot itself show any given dinosaur is an adult.
3. **C.** Sotomayor believes demographic differences between judges can benefit the law and society, as judges with different backgrounds might be able to perceive certain relevant fact patterns others might overlook in order to make more just rulings. Thus, the general public benefits from these rulings and the law itself is not compromised (she still agrees the law must be applied fairly to all).
4. **A.** Because other factors besides volcanic activity could have caused the surface features seen on Titan, the surface features might not reflect (be accurate evidence of) volcanic activity.
5. **D.** If the plants require sufficient light to grow effectively but not excessive heat, evidence that plants in the shade grew better would suggest they were exposed to less thermal stress (stress related to heat).
6. **B.** If the immune systems of birds were strengthened after taking a rest from taxing journeys, this would suggest that the break from migratory strains helped improve the immune systems. The fact that there was no relationship between immune system levels and fat levels suggests that fat levels themselves were not responsible for this boost.
7. **D.** That subjects' responses were more related to whether they believed a painting was fake than to whether the painting was actually fake shows factors other than visual ones affect how the brain processes artwork when one makes aesthetic judgments.
8. **B.** Since brown dwarfs and Jupiter-sized planets look alike and Bennett found more Jupiter-sized planets and fewer brown dwarfs than did Mróz, it is likely Bennett misclassified some brown dwarfs as Jupiter-sized planets, which Mróz later found were actually brown dwarfs.
9. **B.** If Phobos's interior was weaker than previously thought, then tidal waves might actually have been strong enough to cause cracks that they otherwise would not be strong enough to cause if Phobos had a stronger interior, as it was originally believed to have.
10. **A.** Because the characters in comedies are ordinary people dealing with issues common to the human experience, it is likely that many theatergoers can better relate to them.
11. **A.** Because GDP does not account for many measures of economic and personal well-being (such as income inequality and public health related to emissions-related problems), it can be a misleading measure of how people in a country thrive.
12. **C.** The passage suggests the professional networks that lawyers have provide them with a competitive edge in campaigning, such as through better-funded campaigns that can be more effective at swaying voters..
13. **B.** If scholars dismiss Zuckerman as a mere assistant rather than regard her as a co-author, then they downplay (minimize) her contributions to the research on the Matthew Effect.
14. **A.** If the Mycenaeans made use of Egyptian technologies but had minimal direct contact with them, this would suggest an intermediary (another group who did have more contact with the Egyptians) passed Egyptian knowledge to them.
15. **B.** If woodpecker finches can master tool use without social learning, this suggests there is an innate (inborn) component to this not entirely dependent on social learning.

16. **B**. Because the task difficulty was not controlled for (held constant), it is difficult to make valid comparisons about cognitive ability, so the results can be misleading. In order to evaluate the effects of aerobic exercise on cognition, it is essential the tasks used to evaluate cognitive prowess are comparable.

17. **A**. The passage shows that many African nations had their own unique artwork reflecting their own cultural values, but Africans also incorporated European elements based on their interactions with them pre-colonization. Thus, European influence on African art predates colonization.

18. **D**. That the mice without the *Kv.1.3* had a more acute smell after high dilution of odors suggests the expression of this gene diminishes sensitivity to faint smells (those with active genes are less sensitive to dilute odors).

19. **B**. If artifacts with European origins reached regions of the Arctic before colonization, this would suggest the artifacts got there by other means, such as through trade.

20. **C**. Because there is no clear framework for ensuring royalty sharing is fair, advocates for farmers might worry farmers will not be adequately paid. Thus, there may not be an objective third party who can ensure farmers are compensated fairly.

21. **C**. If coconuts existed throughout the globe millions of years ago (before humans existed), this suggests there was an ancient dispersal event that predated human activity.

22. **B**. Because there are multiple viable explanations for what the red daubs could represent and no written evidence clarifying what they mean, we cannot conclusively say they are attributed to the painters witnessing a volcanic eruption.

23. **C**. If maternal DNA has local European lineage and paternal DNA had Middle Eastern lineage, this would suggest Middle Eastern men migrated to Europe and started families with local female populations.

24. **C**. It is difficult to find appropriate control subjects because there is generally no way of knowing in advance which people will and will not become CEOs at large companies.

25. **B**. If corn was not fully domesticated in Mexico 5,000 years ago yet was already in the process of being domesticated elsewhere, the implication is that corn underwent independent domestication events. In other words, it became fully domesticated separately in different locations.

Drill 4

1. **C**. The narrator moved to Chicago from Denver with hopes of a better future, but she found "three weeks the cruelty of indifference" and felt nostalgic for Denver, where she left. The passage suggests her adjustment to Chicago has been difficult.

2. **C**. The excerpt presents a brief overview of how Alexander discovered penicillin as a result of a fortunate accident and why that discovery was important.

3. **B**. The sentence highlights a limitation of the research technique (something the X-ray technology can't do): determine how objects arrived where they did.

4. **D**. The key idea of the poem is that while the Indians may have changed their external behaviors, they have not vanished ("He has changed externally but he has not vanished/ He is an industrial and commercial man, competing with the world; he has not/ vanished.")

5. **A**. The speaker first describes a distinctive sight (the tree with a shadow that seems to touch a house with bricks the color of blood) and then questions what meaning to attribute to that sight (if she is witnessing a hand or a shadow).

6. **A**. The sentence presents a generalization about how non-native species can fulfill an ecological niche. It sets up the example of the red vented bulbul (native to Asia), which accomplished this in Hawaii by dispensing seeds, helping its new ecosystem.

7. **B**. The speaker begins by lamenting flaws he sees in himself and society, calling people in cities and himself foolish and faithless. He ultimately concludes that the good he offers the world is his writing, allowing him to realize his value.

8. **C**. While Thomas anticipates there is a lot in Fanny his family will not like and that he has to be mindful of her influence on his daughters, he concludes that his daughters are old enough that there is likely nothing to worry about. In other words, he does not think introducing Fanny into the family poses a genuine risk to his children.

9. **A**. The speaker expresses both contempt ("Although she feeds me bread of bitterness, And sinks into my throat her tiger's tooth/Stealing my breath of life") and admiration for America ("I love this cultured hell that tests my youth!/Her vigor flows like tides into my blood,/Giving me strength erect against her hate"). He finds America both crushing and invigorating.

10. **C**. The sentence presents a mystery that has puzzled scientists (why some lichens are toxic and others aren't) that the research team ultimately was unable to solve (it found no genetic differences between them).

11. **B**. The passage portrays a character's walk home with her cow and the setting. For example, we are given descriptions of the shady wood, the water, stirrings from the birds overhead, and the softness and sweetness of the air.

12. **A**. The passage makes a claim that the artist Theodora Skipitares makes use of puppets in her works to illuminate important issues. It then gives an example of one play in which she does this (*The Age Of Invention*), which comments on the plights of pioneer women.

13. **C**. The speaker gives advice to his son about how to navigate life. He tells him things he needs to be able to do to be a man, such as maintaining his ability to talk to ordinary people and not letting other people hurt him.

14. **A**. The land is characterized as having ugly moods, suggesting why it presents a difficulty for a character. The land is difficult to manage.

15. **D**. The detail in the underlined sentence supports the idea of the waiters being efficient, or that they work quickly and effectively.

16. **B.** The poem contains an extended comparison, showing how stars are like physical structures, especially buildings (particularly it describes how they are mansions that house spirits).

17. **B.** The sentence describes the methodology, or methods, the researchers used in their study to measure roaming entropy, and it reveals how they correlated this to self-reported emotions.

18. **C.** The passage conveys the contrast between the narrator's initial enchantment with a location ("I had the view of a castle of romance inhabited by a rosy sprite, such a place as would somehow, for diversion of the young idea, take all color out of storybooks and fairytales") where she worked to her distaste for it ("No; it was a big, ugly, antique, but convenient house, embodying a few features of a building still older, half-replaced and half-utilized, in which I had the fancy of our being almost as lost as a handful of passengers in a great drifting ship.")

19. **A.** The poem celebrates the accomplishments of Ethiopians, saying they have the right to "noble pride." He praises them for being noble and forgiving after overcoming injustices. He claims that bards (poets) will celebrate Ethiopia's glory.

20. **B.** The underlined portion gives a specific example of a situation in which Native Americans influenced the suffrage movement by citing how certain activists were inspired by Native women.

21. **C.** The sentence gives a specific example of a behavior (dishonest signaling) carried out by one animal.

22. **A.** The sentence dramatically underscores the narrator's desire to have experiences off of the shore, noting how he leaves for the sea whenever he feels compelled to act violently towards others.

23. **B.** White Fang was initially hostile to being pet. The last sentence shows that Weedon hears "the faintest hint of a croon of content and that none but he could hear," meaning he can sense that White Fang is warming up to him. The sentence hints at the growing emotional bond between Weedon and White Fang.

24. **A.** The passage reveals why caution is needed when making claims that teaching based on learning styles improves learning: Talal's study found no such evidence for this.

25. **B.** Jordan says public servants must do more and offer the people a better vision of the future. Thus, she does not want public officials to grow complacent but to instead strive to be better.

Drill 5

1. **A.** The passage emphasizes that Túpac Amaru II had a notable impact on Peru's history. Thus, he was an important, or **significant**, public figure.
2. **A.** Because of factors that remove evidence of past impacts, physical evidence on Earth today might not indicate, or **reflect**, the history of celestial objects that have hit Earth.
3. **C.** Researchers found a way to move past, or **overcome**, an obstacle for the use of perovskite solar cells.
4. **B.** The sentence is contrasting more obvious signs of burnout with less obvious, or **recognizable**, signs.
5. **B.** The sentence describes the process of obtaining, or collecting, rock samples. Thus, the process can be described as a **collection** process.
6. **C.** Scientists spend time examining, or **inspecting**, small particles.
7. **B.** The sentence contrasts signs of plants that have experienced problems (those that are not healthy) with signs of those that are **healthy.**
8. **C.** A feeling of enthusiasm, or **excitement**, for two passions led to Hartman melding them together.
9. **B.** Scientists **believed**, or had faith in, this conclusion because the evidence was so convincing.
10. **D.** While Congress itself makes laws, it authorizes (gives permission) to independent agencies to carry out, or **implement**, such laws with more specific regulations that align with the laws' specifications.
11. **C.** Because it is versatile, Morse Code enjoys **widespread** (extensive) use by a variety of industries.
12. **A.** Despite evidence that could suggest Marlowe and Shakespeare worked together, other scholars doubt the *Henry VI* plays were a product of **collaboration** (teamwork).
13. **B.** Because there are some efforts underway to build high speed rail, the prediction about it gaining popularity is not completely proven wrong, or **invalidated**, by the cancellation of some such projects.
14. **B.** Although the Iroquois might have had a bigger impact on the Constitution, that does not mean the influence of the Enlightenment was not insignificant, or **unimportant.** This is supported by the idea that the Founders drew inspiration from John Locke.
15. **D.** The description of how the sculptor refashioned household objects shows he was creative, or **inventive.**
16. **C.** The new research shows glial cells have more purposes than was once thought, meaning they are more **versatile**.
17. **B.** Time and resources being wasted exemplifies **inefficiency** (ineffectiveness).
18. **A.** The passage highlights how **intricate** (complex) the relations are between the three parts of the "iron triangle," which help each other in multiple ways.
19. **B.** Some experts **hypothesize** (speculate) that educational interventions will combat digital misinformation, while others speculate that fact-checking technology will be more relevant in this regard.
20. **A.** The change in production was rapid, or **abrupt.**
21. **A.** The meanings are difficult to decode, or **decipher**, which is why they are subject to debate and different interpretations.
22. **D.** Rather than being thoughtless, or **careless**, Stein made intentional choices to violate grammatical rules.

23. **A.** The researchers want to know if the effect of resource limitation is **considerable** (significant) enough to make a difference in reproductive success.
24. **B.** The firm went beyond (did more than merely) **adhere to** (stick to) traditions. It expanded on them by incorporating 21st century amenities.
25. **C.** Traditional models have **surmised** (supposed) that humans are rational economic actors, but behavioral economics challenges this view.
26. **D.** Some experts want to expose (make known) and develop **latent** (undeveloped, or not obvious) talents in children by providing opportunities to those with emerging abilities.
27. **B.** Adjaye becomes **informed** (knowledgeable) about the places where he does his projects.
28. **D.** The evidence shows that compensation and benefits are **eclipsed by** (overshadowed by) importance by other factors that often matter more to employees.
29. **A.** Traditional tools were to used **generate** (produce) paintings, and AI was used to manipulate them.
30. **C.** Henry IV had to fight a Civil War to **buttress** (support) his right to the throne when the legitimacy of his rule was challenged.
31. **A.** Morrison was an **advocate of** (proponent of) Black writers, and she worked to help them get exposure during her tenure at the publishing house.
32. **D. Involuntary** (automatic) movements, such as blinking, can result from TMS.
33. **C.** The study was challenged by findings that Bennett **inaccurately** (incorrectly) classified some stars as planets.
34. **B.** If Smith's efforts are persistent, then it can most reasonably be inferred her lectures are **regular** (recurrent or repeated).
35. **A.** Because climate change is a complex problem, the solutions are not **straightforward** (simple).
36. **A.** Some people think practices that help profit and the environment are not **compatible** (able to coexist harmoniously) because many measures that maximize profits also pollute the environment.
37. **A.** The SDSS is an **illustration** (example) of citizen science.
38. **B.** The passage describes how legumes have **solved** (found a workable solution) to the problems caused by low nitrogen supply.
39. **C.** Brubeck's experimentations show how he refused to **conform to** (adhere to) conventions (traditions).
40. **B.** Fine dining and street food might seem like they cannot **intersect** (overlap) because they seem to exist in their own spheres (domains).
41. **D.** Since many of Buck's books portray farmers, the character of Wang Lung (a farmer) is not **atypical** (unusual).
42. **C.** Noé **repudiated** (rejected) conventions by not including a script.
43. **B.** If the brain of the dodo was **comparable to** (similar to) those of other animals with strong cognitive skills, that would logically lead to the conclusion the dodo might have similar abilities.
44. **B.** The situation in which people have mixed feelings about democracy in theory and in practice shows they are **ambivalent** (conflicted) .
45. **C.** For voters who disapprove of the two major parties, third parties might be a **palatable** (acceptable) alternative.

46. **B.** More vigilant (attentive) monitoring is **warranted** (defensible) because the most vulnerable birds are also the most difficult to track.
47. **B.** The sentence contrasts humor that is superficially (on the surface) **innocuous** (harmless) yet is actually biting (stinging).
48. **A.** Islands away from the mainland are remote, or **peripheral** (in outlying areas).
49. **A.** Carracci's art drew on **disparate** (dissimilar, or distinct) influences.
50. **C.** A **dearth** (a small number) of studies in applied educational settings motivated Wooldridge to conduct one such study.
51. **D.** The protagonist defies **prescribed** (laid down as social rules) traditions by not marrying for social standing, as is customary.
52. **B.** Ortner rejected the idea that culture was **static** (unchanging), instead arguing it was constantly changing.
53. **C.** The contention is **tenuous** (weak). To be more convincing, it needs to address contradictory evidence.
54. **D.** Even people from an **unremarkable** (ordinary) background can make a big difference.
55. **A.** In his absence, Hagar felt a **yearning** (desire) for Milkman's presence, as his absence is painful and bitter for her.
56. **A.** It was once thought women's **domain** (area of expertise) was in the home.
57. **A.** Douglas struggled to **put into words** (verbalize) the emotion he feels.
58. **C.** The team studied if animals can **produce** (create) the appropriate neural activity.
59. **B.** In context, it makes most sense to say that some people fear women's exercise of her **intellectual capacities** (intelligence). By using her reasoning skills and intellect, a woman can act as a reformer who changes society for the better. This would also set up the discussion of why women would not be satisfied with their narrow sphere. They can use their intelligence to expand opportunities for themselves.
60. **C. Fundamental** (foundational) human rights like freedom of speech are easily understood.
61. **B.** The speaker says sorrows might **last** (persist in time) forever.
62. **D.** The American Dream need not be **postponed** (delayed) forever. The fact that Jordan is a speaker at the DNC when at one time that would be unthinkable shows that positive changes can happen.
63. **C.** Gwendolyn feels **obliged** (compelled) to reveal her true feelings.
64. **C.** Model organisms allow us to make comparisons to humans. The ventral nerve cord is **comparable to** (similar to) the spinal cord in humans.
65. **B.** The scene is **peculiar** (odd), from the attempt to convey grace to the appearance of the room. The question "Was this really Italy?" hints that the characters find the scene odd.
66. **A.** Dorian would examine with **meticulous** (thorough) care his signs of aging, which preoccupied him.
67. **A.** Mercy (forgiveness and compassion) is an **attribute** (trait) that is not strained but freely given.
68. **B.** La Follette **affirms** (states) that Congress and the people each have certain powers.
69. **B.** Roosevelt is against **undiscerning** assaults on character, or those that make no distinctions between those who actually did and did not commit corrupt acts. Scoundrels like nothing more than when honest people are assailed (attacked).

70. **A.** It is hard to **infer** (deduce) what the serving girl is thinking (what she is "serving" with just her eyes).
71. **D.** Despite the dark times, Douglass is hopeful America is **pliable** (impressionable) enough at this point in her existence that change can occur.
72. **C.** Time has failed to **destroy** (get rid of) the pyramids built by the South Street men.

Drill 6

1. **A.** The first passage argues that many business owners are hesitant to delegate tasks because they like to be in control. Thus, the author of Text 1 would likely say convincing business owners to adopt the recommendation to delegate tasks (in the last sentence of Text 2) will be challenging.

2. **C.** Text 2 argues that employees are less engaged and thus less productive when they work from home. Thus, this author would likely say that even the most qualified employees would benefit from working in an office.

3. **B.** Mehta does agree that a hyperfocus on grit can detract from social justice issues, but he believes the more salient criticism of grit advocates is that they misunderstand motivation.

4. **B.** The author of Text 2 would consider the sentence about disastrous nuclear accidents alarmist since nuclear power is "relatively safe" and "the risk of accidents is decreasing."

5. **C.** The team would likely agree the theory is plausible (since it is widely accepted and they expected their results to align with it), but it is not supported empirically by their study (not supported by experimental evidence).

6. **B.** The author of Text 1 states that the arts are unaffordable for many private citizens and organizations to fund adequately but believes that there is high demand for art, as it enriches communities and drives tourism. Thus, this author would likely respond to the claim that a lack of private funding signifies a lack of interest in arts by stating that the author of Text 2 conflates (confuses) an inability to afford funding the arts with a lack of demand to consume it.

7. **B.** Riel-Salvatore would dispute the assumption that Neanderthals lacked intelligence, as evidence shows they made advanced tools (which require intelligence) independently.

8. **D.** The author of Text 2 would likely say the effort to revive the extinct species discussed in Text 1 is misguided and wasteful. In general, Text 2 argues that de-extinction efforts would be better diverted to efforts that protect existing species that are in endangered.

9. **C.** The author of Text 2 would likely be skeptical of interventions to help humans by targeting NCoR1 since studies need to be done testing its safety on humans first, as the side effects can be serious.

10. **B.** Ilin and colleagues would likely say France's conclusion is premature, as new evidence suggests solar flares might not preclude the possibility of life on planets surrounding red dwarfs.

11. **A.** The conclusion that the magma mentioned in the underlined sentence formed in low-pressure conditions was based in part on trace element composition analysis. The author of Text 2 notes that these analyses can be unreliable messengers of magma generation depth, meaning it is possible high-pressure magmas will be confused with low-pressure ones in some cases. Thus, the author of Text 1 might misunderstand the meaning of certain chemical signatures.

12. **A.** Conard and Riehl would dispute the idea that farming spread outwardly from a single focal point, as they found evidence it developed independently in different regions.

13. **D.** Caspar would argue that brain size is a fallible indicator of intelligence, as synaptic connections likely matter more. Drawing a conclusion about intelligence based on presumed brain size is overly ambitious.

14. **A.** The author of Text 2 would say that the argument that the judiciary has the power of "merely judgment" understates its power, as in many cases, it is more powerful than the legislature.
15. **D.** The author of Text 2 concedes that there were stylistic differences between *Everything Everywhere All At Once* and other acclaimed films but notes that this does not take away from its intellectual seriousness. It deals with important themes skillfully and resonates with audiences. Thus, it has cinematic worthiness despite its quirks.
16. **D.** The author of Text 2 notes that allowing countries to secede from the United States at will would be an "absurd" organization for government. He asks the rhetorical question if the Founders would really organize the government in this absurd way, with the implied answer being "no." Thus, secession was inconsistent with the Constitution's framers.

17. **B.** The author of Text 2 notes that Hansberry employed deliberate irony to make an insightful social commentary. When she is seen as being intentional in her subtle contradictions rather than unintentionally including them, thematic coherence (unity) can be brought to her work. For example, we can appreciate how she both embraced and critiqued the American Dream simultaneously: she supported it in theory but lamented it had not been completely realized.
18. **C.** Zehr would see Swift's concerns as somewhat overblown (excessive). Though the music industry did lose profits from streaming, there are promising signs they will make up for lost profits in other ways, such as through increased concert sales.
19. **C.** The second author agrees authentic emotions are needed, but believes that they can best be summoned by careful analysis of the script (the text).
20. **C.** Text 2 argues that there are long-term benefits to increasing employee wages despite initial increased costs. That author would likely criticize the student in Text 1 for only looking at short-term losses and encourage the student to look at a more extended timeframe.

Made in the USA
Middletown, DE
30 October 2023

41485492R00102